FINDING YOUR
LEADERSHIP
SOUL

FINDING YOUR
LEADERSHIP
SOUL

What Our Students Can
Teach Us About **Love, Care,**
and **Vulnerability**

CARLOS R. MORENO

Arlington, Virginia USA

2800 Shirlington Road, Suite 1001 • Arlington, VA 22206 USA
Phone: 800-933-2723 or 703-578-9600 • Fax: 703-575-5400
Website: www.ascd.org • Email: member@ascd.org
Author guidelines: www.ascd.org/write

Richard Culatta, *Chief Executive Officer;* Anthony Rebora, *Chief Content Officer;* Genny
Ostertag, *Managing Director, Book Acquisitions & Editing;* Susan Hills, *Senior Acquisitions
Editor;* Mary Beth Nielsen, *Director, Book Editing;* Jennifer L. Morgan, *Editor;* Thomas Lytle,
Creative Director; Donald Ely, *Art Director;* Yassmin Raiszadeh/The Hatcher Group,
Graphic Designer; Circle Graphics, *Typesetter;* Kelly Marshall, *Production Manager;*
Shajuan Martin, *E-Publishing Specialist;* Christopher Logan, *Senior Production Specialist*

All web links in this book are correct as of the publication date below but may have
become inactive or otherwise modified since that time. If you notice a deactivated or
changed link, please email books@ascd.org with the words "Link Update" in the subject
line. In your message, please specify the web link, the book title, and the page number on
which the link appears.

PAPERBACK ISBN: 978-1-4166-3263-4   ASCD product #123025   n12/23
PDF EBOOK ISBN: 978-1-4166-3264-1; see Books in Print for other formats.
Quantity discounts are available: email programteam@ascd.org or call 800-933-2723,
ext. 5773, or 703-575-5773. For desk copies, go to www.ascd.org/deskcopy.

Library of Congress Cataloging-in-Publication Data

Names: Moreno, Carlos R., author.
Title: Finding your leadership soul : what our students can teach us about love, care,
    and vulnerability / Carlos R. Moreno.
Description: Arlington, Virginia USA : ASCD, [2024] | Includes bibliographical references
    and index.
Identifiers: LCCN 2023037724 (print) | LCCN 2023037725 (ebook) | ISBN 9781416632634
    (paperback) | ISBN 9781416632641 (pdf ebook)
Subjects: LCSH: Educational leadership.
Classification: LCC LB2806 .M62 2024 (print) | LCC LB2806 (ebook) | DDC 371.2/
    011–dc23/eng/20230912
LC record available at https://lccn.loc.gov/2023037724
LC ebook record available at https://lccn.loc.gov/2023037725

33 32 31 30 29 28 27 26 25 24   1 2 3 4 5 6 7 8 9 10 11 12

Para Ana y Victoriano—

Nada hubiera sido posible sin su amor y su apoyo. A ustedes le dedico este libro.

Praise for *Finding Your Leadership Soul*

Leading with love is the core of this thoughtful and beautiful narrative. In Moreno's deft hands, this is more than a book about leadership beyond trauma and struggle. It is a story about the near magic of surviving not only to thrive but to bring the ancestors and future generations with you on the journey—and through the journey, make everybody, including oneself, just that much better. I am so grateful for this book in the world.

—**Jacqueline Woodson,** author and National Book Award winner

Despite the plethora of "leadership" courses available in this society, none of them truly moves beyond the intellectual. True leadership is not just a "head" activity. It is also a "heart" and "soul" undertaking. Carlos Moreno's brilliant volume helps readers delve deep into the importance of who we are and what happens when we bring our whole selves to the leadership equation. Let's hope many more education leaders will find their Leadership Soul!

—**Gloria Ladson-Billings,** professor and author of *Culturally Relevant Pedagogy*

In this deeply moving and personal book, Carlos Moreno draws upon his own experiences as a child growing up in the Bronx; as a teacher in Providence, RI; and as national leader of leaders to provide other educators with insights on how to lead with soul. Inspiring, thought-provoking, and authentic, this book offers wisdom and practical guidance to educational leaders. During these uncertain and challenging times, *Finding Your Leadership Soul* is the resource we need.

—**Pedro Noguera,** dean of the Rossier College of Education, University of Southern California

This book is simply beautiful. Each page is filled with the power of vulnerability to heal and manifest justice. I am in awe of how Carlos uses his words to heal. Every Black boy in America needs to read this book, along with every teacher and school leader. After reading this book you will sit in gratitude and return to the text again and again.

—**Bettina Love,** professor and bestselling author of *Punished for Dreaming* and *We Want to Do More Than Survive*

In this wise and compelling book, Carlos Moreno offers readers a two-fer. He shares deeply personal stories and reflections about the true meaning of leadership, and he issues a powerful call to action to reimagine how we lead our classrooms, organizations, and even ourselves. *Finding Your Leadership Soul* will stir you to think big and act boldly.

—**Daniel H. Pink,** New York Times bestselling author of *The Power of Regret, Drive,* and *When*

Written from a deeply empathetic and visionary perspective, Carlos Moreno's *Finding Your Leadership Soul* invites current and emerging leaders to chart a new course—one defined by love, care, and vulnerability. Drawing from a rich tapestry of stories and research, it illuminates the path toward a more authentic and inclusive style of leadership that speaks to the heart of our shared humanity. Through its pages, readers embark on a transformative journey, discovering that the key to impactful leadership lies not in commanding from a distance, but in forging genuine connections that uplift, inspire, and endure.

—**Linda Darling-Hammond,** president, Learning Policy Institute, and professor emerita, Stanford University

Imagine a world where vulnerability isn't just a buzzword—it's the heart and soul of leadership. Carlos Moreno paints a vivid picture through stories that'll hit you right in the gut about his own leadership journey, one informed by trauma, love, and growth. *Finding Your Leadership Soul* is as powerful and inspiring as they come, equally insightful and uplifting. No matter where you may be on your leadership pathway, it's worth taking a pause to infuse some soul.

—**Blair Underwood,** Emmy Award–winning actor, activist, and philanthropist

Finding Your Leadership Soul is Carlos Moreno's deeply authentic story of leading as his true self and all that comes with that. In this book, "Los" delivers an important narrative on how his personal lived experiences have allowed him to lead in multiple spaces and places. This book will help education leaders as well as leaders across multiple sectors recognize how your personal journey informs and orders your leadership steps. These are the important lessons needed to propel our nation forward. The Bronx is proud!!

—**Meisha Porter,** former chancellor, NYC Schools, and CEO of The Bronx Community Foundation

Author and educator Carlos Moreno allows us to bear witness to the journey of so many of our nation's Black and Latino males, who travel to manhood in urban settings and in educational environments that rob them of their innocence, steal their joy, and ensure their failure in school and in life. In this moving reflection, a powerful counter-narrative is illuminated, fueled by the love of families and influential individuals [to show ways to] bridge the gap between hopeless futures and lives lived with purpose and meaning. *Finding Your Leadership Soul* is a must-read—not just because of the youthful traumas so painfully depicted but most especially because of the hope, resilience, and success portrayed, which we collectively can and must ensure for the young people under our watch.

—**Deborah Jewell-Sherman,** professor for education leadership, Harvard Graduate School of Education

Finally, a book not from a researcher or policymaker but from a leader-practitioner who tells it like it really is when it comes to working with youth while centering love, care, and vulnerability. In *Finding Your Leadership Soul,* Carlos Moreno's letters to parents, family members, and students, along with his use of research, are a breath of fresh air that will make a stone cry. A must-read that requires you to think with your body but feel with your mind! This is a big part of a new way forward.

—**Elliot Washor,** author of *Learning to Leave* and cofounder of Big Picture Learning

Carlos Moreno's *Finding Your Leadership Soul* demonstrates the best of reflective and reflexive writing, courageously blending compelling memoir with sobering empirical research. As a reader, you are taken on a journey—comprising a subway ride, a slow-paced walk, and, at times, a run—with a young man of color coming of age while navigating the neighborhoods, historical challenges, and changes in New York City, a richly diverse metropolis with the largest school district in the country. Carlos personalizes the political, embodying through his narrative what we wave away as statistics or an intractable "problem" in our communities, to reclaim the importance of embracing all our young people as exceptional, not the exception, to retrain our eye on trying to change structures, not students. This book is a clarion call for leaders to find the individual and collective courage to transform our institutions, embrace young people for who they are, and convert love into action that fuels the quest for justice and not just order in a world in great need of it.

—**Noel S. Anderson,** clinical professor of
educational leadership and policy studies, New York University

As a fellow Black educator with immigrant roots from the Bronx, NY, I connect deeply with Carlos Moreno's *Finding Your Leadership Soul,* which speaks to many of the challenges and triumphs I faced as a student, educator, and teacher educator. Through stories from his experiences as a grandson, son, father, friend, educator, and leader, Moreno captivates his readers and takes us with him on his journey to Leadership Soul. This book not only provides educators with an example of finding power in ourselves and giving ourselves grace, but also reminds us to lead with love, care, and vulnerability. *Finding Your Leadership Soul* is the balm our education system needs now.

—**Dena N. Simmons,** founder, LiberatED

Informed by his own life journey, Carlos Moreno offers a framework for the authentic, humane, and unconditional care our most marginalized students deserve. A must-read if you are looking for insight and inspiration on how to make a lasting difference in the lives of these young men (and women).

—**Kent McGuire,** director of education programs,
The William and Flora Hewlett Foundation

In a truly personal and accessible tone and with no holds barred, Moreno shares his leadership journey as a Black, Latino male from the Bronx centering three pillars: love, care, and vulnerability. This book is a love letter not only to other Black and Latino male educators he seeks to call into the profession but to our entire education sector.

—**Nancy Gutiérrez,** president and lead executive officer, The Leadership Academy

Finding Your Leadership Soul brought me to full attention. This compelling read is an authentic testimonial that provides an internal look into the process by which Carlos was being healed to triumph over trauma and revived to answer his soul's call to lead. Unlike other leadership books filled with technical remedies, this book brings the reader in touch with the reality of finding one's mission by first finding and believing in oneself.

—**Ron Walker,** executive director, The Coalition of Schools Educating Boys of Color

If you believe education leadership should be grounded in love, care, and vulnerability, you need this book. But if you think education leadership should be centered on standardization, discipline, and assessment . . . *you need this book even more!*

—**Sam Seidel,** coauthor of *Hip-Hop Genius 2.0, Creative Hustle,* and *Changing the Conversation About School Safety*

We find ourselves in the midst of a paradigm shift in education. Historically, previous radical changes in the education system still marginalized and deprioritized our most vulnerable students. Moreno's *Finding Your Leadership Soul* readjusts our focus by reminding us not to continue to neglect the voices of Black and Brown boys and men as we reimagine our leadership. I'm proud to say Moreno's work, *Finding Your Leadership Soul,* adds to my joy.

—**Sharif El-Mekki,** CEO, Center for Black Educator Development

Carlos Moreno has never shied away from embracing love, care, and vulnerability—critical underpinnings of humanity—as the core principles of his leadership style. This, among so many other reasons, is why I'm proud to call him a friend. *Finding Your Leadership Soul,* a book filled with bold, universal truths destined to have a broad impact on today's fragile world, is a song of inspiration to a coming generation of Black and Brown men and women who see themselves as emerging leaders.

—**Deborah Quazzo,** managing partner, GSV Ventures

Finding Your Leadership Soul by Carlos Moreno needs to be read now . . . by everyone. The letters to students are so raw and real. Through these letters, Carlos brings the importance of love, care, and vulnerability to the forefront. These are not just words but are brought to life by real-life examples. Imagine if schools were built on love, care, and vulnerability. Carlos has become an incredible leader who opens up to readers about his own growth through this book. Start reading now!

—**Dennis Littky,** cofounder of Big Picture Learning,
The Met High School, and College Unbound

Through this profoundly beautiful and powerful book, Carlos Moreno has penned a love letter to Black and Brown boys and to those who care about and for them. It's a love letter to humanity and a journey through healing, reflection, becoming, and evolving for all who are called to the work and practice of leadership. It is the loving, caring, and vulnerable call to action for us to do better so that Black and Brown children—and all students, by extension—are seen, protected, affirmed, and supported in the fullness of their being, genius, interests, and needs. At a time when all facets of society are under attack and the future of education feels gloomy, *Finding Your Leadership Soul* is the fuel and the hope needed to anchor and orient us. A must-read!

—**Gislaine Ngounou**, former president and CEO, Nellie Mae Education Foundation

Carlos Moreno speaks his truth through every word on the page and exemplifies how one can always find light in the darkness. The light serves as his guide, and his dedication is shown through his impact as an educator. His servant leadership is on full display, and you see how this colossal educator has become the beacon of hope he is today. Carlos is telling stories that often go untold, and that is what makes *Finding Your Leadership Soul* so powerful.

—**Naseem Haamid,** law student, University of the District of Columbia,
and Big Picture Learning graduate from the Bronx

FINDING YOUR
LEADERSHIP
SOUL

**What Our Students Can
Teach Us About Love, Care,
and Vulnerability**

Foreword: On Leading, Becoming, and Soul

Titles like "leader" and "leadership" are often used to describe a trait or position that denotes power. The aspiration for any person who enters a field of study or profession is to one day become or be seen as a leader or part of the leadership. In business and political spheres, leadership consists of the decision makers and power holders. They are the ones the others answer to, but also the people who hold a responsibility for the operating or maintaining of a system. In a world that emphasizes the notion that "not all are called to lead," or that only the special or chosen get to lead, there is a certain universality to the aspiration to leadership. At the same time, leading as a goal or destination for all based on a model for leadership that is about amassing power cannot work in fields like education. In our field, individual power runs in direct opposition to our work. The chief goals of education—to incite passion for learning and allow children to uncover their gifts as they develop into citizens who can engage fully in a democratic world—is less about collecting power and more about distributing it.

Leadership in education requires very different traits, dispositions, and attributes than leadership in any other field. However, because of the universality of "leadership" and the collective pursuit of title, many education leaders—superintendents, principals, assistant principals, teacher leaders—bring noneducation strictures and ideologies to education work. Today—particularly after the pandemic—the fear of losing time, missing opportunities, and assessing what children do not know (instead of what they do not have) has led to an infatuation with measuring and quantifying knowledge in a way that blindly adopts corporate models of leading that distort what leadership in education should be. Business/corporate, political, and other power-amassing models and structures will not improve education. Leadership that is a means to a title and power cannot function well in a field that requires giving that power to students.

To harness and then distribute power to youth—especially the most vulnerable youth—is not something that most people have the capacity to do. There is a certain selflessness and vulnerability required. There is also a particular kind of study of oneself that is necessary. To teach or lead in the key of life first requires some deep innervisions. One does not arrive at leadership with a title, credential, or position. One engages in the process of becoming a leader by understanding the power of sharing power. To lead in education is to be a conduit through which power flows to those historically robbed of it. Leadership is understanding the complications that come with being the vessel for empowering. It is knowing how some will receive it, how others will reject it, how some may leverage it, and how some may be intimidated by it.

This is why leaders in the field of education must always be in the process of becoming.

Becoming a leader in education involves recognizing that the leader is the conduit through which power is transferred to students. It is an ever-evolving, never-ending process of making sure that the soul is intact and prepared to give to students what the ego wants to keep for itself. The soul-centered leadership that Carlos Moreno outlines and describes in this work requires a deliberate process of looking inward (innervisions); focusing outward and on the present (being in the key of life); and releasing tensions, histories, and traumas that inhibit the creation of radical possibilities for (em)powered students. Greene (1978) describes this process as "living with one's eyes open" (p. 43) and concurrently facing inward and outward, or existing in a state of wide-awakeness. Soul leadership is about being vigilant in looking outward, but also living with one's mind's eye or inner eye open. We see this process described throughout *Finding Your Leadership Soul* as Moreno tells stories of both his childhood and his leadership roles. Through letter writing and deep reflection, we see evidence of soul work and becoming in real time.

On the 1973 album *Innervisions*, Stevie Wonder gives an example of the complex work of activating innervisions, or the path to becoming. The album, which covers issues that range from love to politics, has been described as "Wonder's attempt to wrest a measure of hope" within "the rapidly changing conditions in Black America" (Werner, 2004, p. 114). This, in many ways, is the work of school leadership. It is to offer hope to youth by allowing them access to power in a world that disempowers. The soul awakening or becoming is activated in personal reflection, radical vulnerability, and artistic/musical expression. Through Moreno's letters and reflections, we see how becoming and soul work in leadership is done. Through radical vulnerability and truth telling, one clears the space to be a vessel for something bigger than the self. We feel the pain of having your jacket stolen, know the anguish of losing a student, understand the challenges of making the wrong decisions, and witness the power of owning one's history to make sense of one's present.

A soul-centered leadership is particularly important for connecting with Black and Latino boys who have been robbed of their capacity to be vulnerable. The only way for children who have been trained to be on guard at all times to be vulnerable is to be able to witness vulnerability from someone who looks like them. However, the world has conditioned education leaders and teachers to believe that too much emotion hampers their effectiveness and that emotion is a weakness. This same world has stripped feeling from the existence of Black and Latino children—celebrating toughness and bravado at the expense of full representations of their humanity. Black boys, in particular, are put in schools that render them powerless unless they become violent hypermasculine caricatures of who they really are. They enter the world as the prey of the state and, consequently, for the sake of survival, respond in ways intended to scare off a system that hunts them.

I have written and spoken in a number of settings about the deimatic behavior in certain children in response to schools that disempower and attack their spirits. Deimatic behaviors in animals are responses to a threat. If the animal is threatened, it enacts certain behaviors or practices that are designed to intimidate predators and dissuade or distract them from attacking. As Moreno states in this masterful work, "Being Black, Latinx, and from the Bronx bring with them assumptions of poverty, limited opportunities, crime, and violence. As a group, Black and Latino males are often pathologized as unmotivated and academically disinterested." The reality is that they are none of those things. The conditions they are placed in (often reinforced and exacerbated by school leadership) make deimatic behaviors a necessity for survival. Leadership Soul is a disrupting force to the cycle of targeting and punishing youth. In its absence, the tough love that drives deimatic responses persists, and leaders become pseudo wardens in schools that incarcerate minds and souls.

Our collective responsibility, if we are to change the world as leaders in education, is to heed the lessons in this work. To read the stories and the stories within them. To fill in the gaps with what shifted with Angel and what love is with Bella. To see self in both Carlos and Shawn. To imagine what our work could be if we refused to hoard power and decided instead to offer it to those who will one day inherit the Earth.

—**Chris Emdin, PhD**
Robert A. Naslund Endowed Chair in Curriculum Theory
and professor of education, University of Southern California;
author, *For White Folks Who Teach in the Hood . . .
and the Rest of Y'all Too*

To My Younger Self (Age 15)

Mi fuerte Carlito,

<u>I know you.</u> And I know that a terrible thing just happened to you. Two men—men who could have been your uncle, friend, or neighbor—brazenly and violently assaulted you and stole your jacket—a jacket that was meaningful to you not because of the bright Cincinnati Bengals logo stitched to the back (in fact, you don't even like the Bengals!), but because of the sacrifice your mom made to get it for your birthday.

These men didn't just steal your jacket—they also robbed you of your innocence. At the time, neither you nor they could have fully appreciated the vulnerability and fear introduced in that moment and how it would define you. As happens with so many Black and Brown teenage boys, this altercation—lasting only five minutes, though it felt like eternity—catapulted you from a boy to a man in an instant, though mostly not in ways that were positive.

Nearly 30 years later, I want to share what I have learned so that you can continue being a teenager who is cool enough to spin records and DJ from your fourth-floor bedroom window for everyone on the block while also playing Antonio in <u>The Merchant of Venice</u>. You are talented and creative; music and Shakespeare make you happy. Do not allow those men and that moment to take these things away. I want to extend the love and care that the adults in your life should have provided in the aftermath of this trauma. They shouldn't have assumed everything was OK when you showed clear and painful signs of having been harmed.

<u>I see you.</u> I see the scars. I see the tears that you do not shed in public but that flow at night when you're in bed. I am here to allow you to be vulnerable—to share your feelings of fear and frustration. And while I wish that you had not felt the need to turn to people who do not share your values for protection, I understand. You feel safe with them. They assure you that no one will ever lay hands on you like that again.

Please know that I want you to experience joy—you deserve joy— Black boy joy, the type of joy that only comes from allowing yourself to love and be loved. You deserve pure, unconditional love, and you should love unconditionally and purely. This love will fuel your spirit in ways that you simply cannot imagine.

Think of the love you have for Grandma Isabel. I know it's hard to feel it because you can only imagine having conversations with her while standing at her doorway, since you always have something cooler to do than sit down with her. Trade that feeling of impatience for an appreciation of her strength and wisdom. As you mature, Grandma Isabel will be your biggest and most vocal cheerleader. She will brag about you even when there's really nothing to brag about. You will come to understand how much she has sacrificed to ensure that our family could be where they are today. A time will come when you are able to return a small portion of the love and care she shows to you and so many others in our family. She will remain the matriarch of our family until she is overcome by a deadly virus that will kill more than a million Americans and millions more around the world. Until her death, she will be loved and cared for by family and friends, because she loved so many. She will also experience unselfish love in the form of service from care providers who will risk their lives for her.

Embrace her. Celebrate her. Shower her with love.

I want you to know that, while the Bronx seems like a deplorable place to you, Grandma will live here until she passes. Mom and Dad, most of your siblings, and most of your beloved nieces and nephews will remain there, too. And there will soon be a handful of amazing political figures who truly represent the Bronx in beautiful and truthful ways: former New York City Schools' Chancellor Meisha Ross Porter, U.S. Representatives Jamaal Bowman and Ritchie Torres—even a Latina Supreme Court justice, Sonia Sotomayor. The Bronx is representing! If you stay strong and do not give into fear, you will be added to this roster of notable figures.

I implore you to embrace love. Love comes in many forms. Look for it to come to you from a caring and committed community member. Ms. Cheryl Williams will see in you what you are struggling to see in yourself. Allow her to guide you. She will open doors, erect fences, and embrace you, but only if you allow her to care for you. Do that. You deserve to be cared for and to feel safe.

By the time you reach my age, you will have become an educator. You will have the joy and privilege of helping young people live their fullest lives and dreams. You will do so with care, compassion, and commitment—in part because of your relationship with Cheryl. She gets credit for our watchful eye and our ability to reach the students who are pulling the furthest away—the ones who need the strongest embrace.

It is often the loudest, toughest, and scariest among us who are the most susceptible to emotional harm—that's why they protect themselves so strongly. The guys who robbed you were fearful of physical harm, so they carried guns. But please know that you need not follow that path. There are too many young boys like you who believe this path is their only option. As a result, too many Black and Brown boys are being expelled, incarcerated, or worse. I don't want that for you. I don't want that for us.

Over time, you will learn how to be vulnerable. It will begin with you embracing the feeling of being different. It is perfectly OK for you to want to spend time with Mr. Kelly, the only Black male teacher at your school. Only 2 percent of teachers nationwide are Black men. Allow yourself to ask questions and get to know him. Let your curiosity fuel and lead you. As an educator, each relationship you will have with each student will be special, but you will be uniquely appreciative of the relationships you forge with a few of your Black and Brown male students. You and they both will recognize and appreciate the rarity of those opportunities. Trust me: drop your cool veneer and spend time with Mr. Kelly. You both will value it.

Your ancestors are watching and protecting you, Carlito. They will place people along your life's path to guide you when you need it most. Recognize and respect them and allow them to guide you. Life is an exceptional teacher. To understand it, you must live it, which includes learning from those around you.

I love and admire the young man that you are, and I hope you think the same of the man you will become.

Que Dios te cuide,

Carlos

1 | My Leadership Journey

In the grand scheme of things, the loss of a jacket was inconsequential. Rather, it was the harsh and violent way it was taken, the humiliation, and the physical harm that mattered. The injustice and unfairness were profound. In the aftermath of the assault, I was overcome with feelings of shame. The psychological and physical trauma had a hold on me. Like my outside injuries, my insides were raw, exposed, and bloody. Yet the harshest blow was that the world around me continued just as it had before. I was expected to respond as though everything were normal, to ignore the visible and invisible injuries and go right back to being a high school student. The bells still rang and students still crowded the hallways, unaware of the violation I had suffered. The police showed not a hint of anything that resembled sympathy. There was no search for the perpetrators, just a paltry incident report. It was only at home that the empathy I so deeply yearned for was amply provided. There, safe in the care of my loved ones, I could truly begin to heal.

Trauma therapist Resmaa Menakem (2017) examines the impact of traumatic events on both individuals and future generations if the trauma is left untreated. When we respond to trauma with the most wounded parts of ourselves, become cruel or violent, or run away, we experience "dirty pain" (p. 20)—and that pain can be transferred to other people, exacerbating feelings of anger, violence, and mistrust. In attempting to avoid pain and discomfort, we create more of it for ourselves and others. To heal collectively, we must be willing to engage in and feel "clean pain"—to slow down, drop into our bodies, and learn how we are responding to our present moment. Menakem is careful to acknowledge that trauma is not destiny, but survivors with unhealed trauma are better served by a mindfulness of their own response to that trauma. We don't need to be perfect or calm all the time, but it is important to understand the history of our responses so that we can engage in our lives with presence and vulnerability.

If I hadn't had the love and support of my family, how might my trauma have shaped my destiny differently? I believe that the robbery of my jacket was a profound and revelatory moment in my development that transformed the way I looked at the world. I did not want this trauma to be what defined me. I wanted to take what helped me heal and have those healing influences shape the way I looked at the world in positive ways.

I think often about the daily traumas experienced by so many students. What about the young people who don't even have a jacket to steal? What about the students without homes to go to or families who can lavish affection and care on them? What about the scores of young people who still report that they don't have even one trusted adult at their school they could go to for help? It is imperative that we find ways to reach our youth and provide the support that they so desperately seek.

We know that teachers who share some of the same lived experiences as their students better understand their needs. And that school leaders who have close connections with their school's communities can better advocate for their students based on deep understanding (Callahan, 2020). Tragically, there is a dearth of educators who fit this description in schools across the nation. According to National Center for Education Statistics data for 2017–2018, white women make up the vast majority of teachers—79 percent, compared to only 7 percent for Black teachers and 9 percent for Latinx teachers. Simply put, too few students in too few schools are able to see themselves in their educators, and this is particularly true of Black and Brown male students, who together make up between 10 and 11 percent of the national student body (NCES, 2023).

Even before they enter school, Black and Brown boys face many issues that negatively affect their life trajectories. Issues of racism begin in utero. According to the National Partnership for Women & Families (2018), Latinas have a higher birth rate nationwide than white or Black women and a slightly lower maternal mortality rate than white women, but they still do not receive adequate prenatal care or nonmedical support throughout and following childbirth. And Black mothers are more likely to receive subpar care and experience higher mortality rates before, during, and after delivery (Taylor, 2020). Black boys are subject to higher mortality rates—and in far too many cases their prospects remain grim as they grow older. Even as life expectancies for all people in the United States have nearly doubled over the past century, the life expectancy for Black males has persistently lagged behind all other subgroups (Bond & Herman, 2016).

Too often, the words *Black, Latinx,* and *the Bronx* bring with them assumptions of poverty, limited opportunities, crime, and violence. As a group, Black and Latino males are often pathologized as unmotivated and academically disinterested, with bleak prospects and few opportunities. It is not likely that a young Afro-Caribbean boy from the Bronx would be provided with opportunities to develop the tools necessary to achieve success, including high-quality learning experiences in school. Schools in the Bronx and other major urban communities have been historically underfunded and underresourced, with limited access to postsecondary experiences. For these reasons, we tend to celebrate the young men who "make it out." We laud their accomplishments because they are seen as exceptional. *Why don't we do the same for the young men who stay?* We must stop assuming that the labels that many in our society place upon these young people truly describe their potential.

Growing up, I had no intention of pursuing a leadership role in education. If someone had told me that I was going to become a teacher, I would have laughed! How many 6-foot-8 Black male teachers have you seen? I did not feel that I belonged at the head of a classroom.

Or did I? Could it be that my experience growing up as a young Afro-Latino boy in the Bronx would be beneficial? That students who looked like me, were raised like me, and had similar trajectories needed an educator like me? And that I needed them?

My Life in the Bronx

To understand me as a teenager, you must understand the Bronx in the 1960s. My neighborhood shaped who I was to become nearly as much as my family and others I encountered during that time did. Prior to the 1960s, the Bronx was one of the fastest-growing urban areas in the world. It served as an enclave for second-generation immigrants who were escaping the overcrowded neighborhoods of Manhattan. While the Bronx was typical of large urban cities undergoing significant changes, it was also a special place. According to Evelyn Gonzalez (2004), it was "famous for its stable ethnic neighborhoods and housing units [that] on average were better than those of Brooklyn and Manhattan" (p. 5).

The 1960s saw large-scale change in the Bronx, with its demographics evolving dramatically due to white flight, redlining, housing shortages, public housing, and growing urbanization of the borough. By the 1970s, any mention of the Bronx elicited images of burned-out buildings and lawlessness. "Most assessments of the devastation of the 1960s and 1970s emphasize race, crime, poverty, [construction of] the Cross-Bronx Expressway, and Co-op City and ignore a century of urban growth in the Bronx," writes Gonzalez. "Yet it is this ongoing urbanization and neighborhood change that helps explain the devastation and consequent revival that occurred" (p. 5).

According to Gonzalez, what happened in the Bronx was by design: rapid urbanization through construction patterns and building development corralled residents into a densely populated area. Research on the Bronx in the 1970s and 1980s is limited, and most of it focuses on the abysmal living conditions of the South Bronx. There is little to no mention of how communities were built and sustained or how schooling impacted the growing Black and Latinx communities.

The 1970s and 1980s were tumultuous times for all of New York City, but especially for the Bronx. New York was at its lowest point in the 1970s thanks to a serious fiscal crisis accompanied by an overall decline in safety. Subways were dangerous. Murders, rapes, burglaries, and car thefts reached record-setting numbers. Even relatively prosperous sections of the Bronx such as Pelham Bay, Locust Point, and Riverdale did not escape the general malaise. The poor economy affected public services throughout the city.

For the roughly 30 percent of the Bronx that is labeled the "South Bronx," the situation was even worse. Indeed, the 1970s were labeled the "decade of fire," with 7 South Bronx census tracts losing about 97 percent of their buildings to fire and abandonment and an additional 44 tracts losing about half of their buildings (Ricciulli, 2019). The South Bronx was the literal and figurative "hot spot," its reputation cemented as much by folktales as by hard data (Mahler, 2006). While Bronx neighborhoods well to the north were relatively safe, it was still quite easy to watch the burning South Bronx from a rooftop in Riverdale and feel the threat (Diaz, 2011).

Growing up in New York City, I was surrounded by Black and Latinx folks, and they all looked like me. I did not pay much attention to my identity until I entered middle school, where it was brought to my attention by my peers. I was relatively sheltered from having to decide who I was up until that point; I did not need to decide if I was Black *or* Latino. Around middle school and high school, I gravitated toward my fellow Dominicans and Puerto Ricans, but I was always the darkest one in the group. I remember at different times feeling as though I did not have full acceptance from my Latinx friends due to my Afro-Latino appearance.

When I started kindergarten, I spoke only Spanish. I was placed in bilingual classes, where I remained until 3rd grade. When I was growing up, you were either Black or Puerto Rican; no one really tried to understand the nuances and differences of Latinidad. Yet here I was, a Dominican child who primarily spoke Spanish, when most kids who looked like me already spoke English.

I think that this was the beginning of the labeling and grouping I experienced in my schooling. English learners often face achievement and attainment gaps in their learning (Umansky & Dumont, 2021) due in large part to teacher perceptions and formal classification as English learners (ELs). The foundation for my K–12 trajectory was laid as soon as I was labeled EL. Researchers suggest that students in bilingual classrooms are often framed in a deficit manner—they are seen for what they are unable to do rather than what they have the potential to do (Cross, 2020; Gutiérrez & Orellana, 2006). As students, ELs are too often considered problems that need fixing (Gutiérrez & Orellana, 2006), which can lead to negative experiences. These students are often tracked into general or special education classes (Kanno & Kangas, 2014), placed in classes with less skilled teachers (Gandara et al., 2003), and, in the long term, negatively impacted and provided with fewer academic opportunities (Umansky & Dumont, 2021).

While in elementary school at Public School 246, I had one male teacher, Mr. Montalban. He probably had the greatest impact on my learning. His 3rd grade class was the first time I'd been taught in a nonbilingual classroom. In fact, at that point I was placed in gifted and talented (G&T) classes, which lasted until 6th grade. I owe my placement in G&T classes to Mr. Montalban, who advocated for me and believed in my academic abilities and intelligence.

However, after I graduated from elementary school to junior high, it was all downhill. No one cared that I had been in G&T classes at

P.S. 246. None of the teachers and administrators in junior high school (and, later, high school) looked like me or my elementary classmates. It was apparent that they had already made up their minds about who we were as students, and they made little investment in guaranteeing our academic success. I was not being academically challenged, and my teachers were not paying attention to my strengths. I was, after all, just another Black kid from the Bronx.

And it wasn't just my skin color. By the time I was 10 years old, I was taller, bigger, and stronger than all of my friends and most of the teachers. This earned me the nickname "Big Man," which I loved. "Big Man" was never a descriptor for my attitude or behavior; I was a well-behaved and well-mannered kid. However, looking back on my childhood, I experienced adultification much sooner than I would have liked. There was an expectation from adults—mostly teachers— that I needed to be tougher, more mature, and more serious as a young child rather than the silly, energetic, goofy kid that I was. I liked to laugh and be playful. Joy should not be stripped from a young person simply because they happen to be taller and larger than their peers.

Unfortunately, this happens to many Black and Latino boys, who are often stereotyped and viewed with contempt, resulting in negative and often traumatic experiences. "Historically, Black men have endeavored to counter the oppressive stereotypes that proclaim them as all body and no mind, bucks and beasts, monsters, and demons," writes Dancy (2014). "However, nonviolent Black males continue to face a world that sees them as violent" (p. 51). My Latino identity also triggered adultification. In school, there were expectations of how a Brown boy should behave, and concepts such as *machismo* influenced how I was treated by teachers and my peers.

Somewhat ironically, I got bullied in elementary school. A lot. I seldom had problems with anyone my size; it was often the smaller kids who challenged me. Perhaps they harbored inferiority complexes. Why they took it out on me, I will never understand, but I knew that I did not want to fight. As the bullying persisted, I was forced to defend myself. Thankfully, Mr. Montalban stepped in. He understood that he could not be in all places at once. Fights were bound to happen when he could not be there. So he did the next best thing. He taught me not only how to stand up for myself, but how to throw a punch. I found an advocate in him. He pushed me to excel academically, showing me that I could be more than my track. But the biggest gift he gave me was a love for chess. I can only speculate, but I think he wanted me to know that I did not always have to focus on my size or appearance and that I could be a strategic thinker. He treated me with love and care and allowed me to be my most vulnerable, when so many others only saw me as "Big Man."

My Bronx Angel

I experienced the clearest and most profound examples of love, care, and vulnerability after a traumatic event a couple of months after I was robbed of my jacket at gunpoint. One day, while on my way home from high school, I witnessed a close friend get shot and killed about 100 meters from where I was walking. For quite some time, I was terrified and scared for my own life. My fear was rooted in my connection to the victim; after all, he was my friend. But it was because I saw who shot him that I thought, *That could have been me.*

It changed everything. I avoided crowds. Never took the same way home from school. For a while, I did not want to leave my house. I was scared to open the door. When the doorbell rang, I became paranoid. Suddenly, there were people in my neighborhood I did not trust. Because the shooting took place two blocks from my home, the shooter had to know who I was, right? I started to feel secure only in the safe space of school. I took comfort in sports and cultivated my appreciation for Shakespeare (which had been sparked by my 6th grade teacher, Mrs. Losak). In school, I felt that I could be who I'd been before I witnessed my friend's death.

It was during this time that I met Cheryl, the woman who would release me from the dread and fear that I faced daily. Cheryl worked in my neighborhood and, as luck would have it, her office was right across the street from my apartment building. She was a community organizer and youth outreach director for the Fordham-Bedford satellite office of the Northwest Bronx Community and Clergy Coalition. This group supported people in the community primarily by helping them access affordable rent, but they also organized protests, worked closely with clergy, and linked young people to opportunities. Part of Cheryl's role was to put together events such as basketball games, form recreational teams, and assist young people looking for jobs and internships. I immediately took to Cheryl. She was a Black woman, short, dark-skinned, and, in her own words, "tomboy-ish." Most of the other community workers were white graduates from Fordham University, but Cheryl looked like me. She understood me.

One day, while I was sitting on my stoop, she approached me and said, "Your name is Carlos, right?" She had seen me around the neighborhood—as a 6-foot-5 15-year-old, I was hard to miss. She asked me lots of questions and eventually said, "You want to do something different? Do you want a job?" I felt like a huge load was being lifted. Someone actually *saw* me! I was being offered a way out!

You see, when Cheryl asked if I wanted to do something different, she meant something beyond hanging out and making money alongside the hustlers on my block—guys I'd grown up around but never really wanted to spend time with because of the dangers that came with their lifestyle. But with those dangers came safety as well—and at the age of 15, I had already been assaulted and robbed at gunpoint and witnessed one of my close friends being murdered. Being around these guys gave me a simulated sense of safety that I had only found at home or at school.

I took Cheryl up on her offer.

This was just before the summer of my junior year. I had never had a real job before. Cheryl helped me and some other kids from the block fill out our applications for the city's Summer Youth Employment Program. She even accompanied me and another kid from my neighborhood to Brooklyn to hand in our applications. I landed a job doing cleanup work in a park near the Bronx River. And every two weeks, when it was time to pick up our checks, she came with us. She never sent us out on our own, as it was known that, too often, kids were being robbed of their summer youth program checks immediately after picking them up.

In my senior year of high school, when I could not work as much because of my sports commitments, Cheryl still found a way to keep me occupied. She paid me and my two best friends to do some building maintenance and cleanup at her building on Seabury Place in the South Bronx. It was in those in-between times that she really showed me what care looked like. It was in the way she would cook for and feed us; the way she taught me to embrace my Blackness, my Afro-Latinidad, and my history, which she knew better than I did; the way she lovingly and aggressively corrected my grammar. She even taught me how to play Spades—a rite of passage in the Black community. She also helped me with one essential task that my high school did not: applying to college. I had no idea what colleges were looking for, but with great patience and attention to detail, we completed my applications. Though she was not a formal teacher, she was the best educator I have ever had.

In the summer before I headed off to college, Cheryl helped me and my two best friends, Ron and Damon, get work at a Black-owned daycare in the Sedgwick Houses projects. Imagine the sight of three Black 17-year-olds, all above 6 foot 4, working with 3- to 5-year-olds! One thing stuck out to us at this daycare: we seldom saw dads picking up their children. That fact gave me pause. Cheryl noted the lack of father involvement, too, and I think that is why she placed us there. She knew we could make a difference. When I reflect on my experiences at the daycare, I often wonder how many of those 3- to 5-year-olds ever saw another Black male educator. Unbeknownst to me, Cheryl had planted a seed—one that would take some time to sprout but would eventually lead me to the classroom.

Cheryl helped to alleviate the fear and dread that I felt following my friend's death. She invested in my potential, which had been mostly ignored in my primary and secondary schooling experiences. She guided my processing of current events taking place in our city and around the world, helped me with challenging school assignments, and reviewed my earliest writings, providing me with tremendously affirming and useful feedback. There were lessons throughout my interactions with Cheryl that I would later understand were all tied to love, care, and vulnerability.

My College Experience

I knew that I would leave the Bronx and even New York one day. It had to happen. In my mind, I could not achieve all that I wanted to if I stayed in the same place. Before I was even thinking about college, I would visit my sister, her husband, and my niece and nephew at their home in Providence, Rhode Island, and think, *This is close enough, and also far enough away.*

Rhode Island was quiet, clean, and definitely *not* the Bronx. When the time came to start thinking about college, I looked to my strengths as a student-athlete to guide my decisions. While I played multiple sports, I was most passionate about basketball. I was scouted by several colleges, including Johnson & Wales University, located in Providence, which at the time was starting a Division III basketball program. Images of Providence from my time spent there came rushing back. This would be my school—where I would start my life outside New York.

As I was growing up, my parents made sure that I was deeply loved and cared for, and this love extended into my college years. I was accepted to Johnson & Wales University and received a great financial aid package, but it did not cover all my expenses, and I needed a loan to cover the remaining cost of my education. As a 17-year-old, I did not have the means to get a loan beyond my already guaranteed Stafford loans.

My father is old-school. He believes in paying for everything in cash and owing no one anything ever. I was gearing up to do some serious convincing, but I didn't have to say much. He simply said,

"Si eso es lo que tenemos que hacer, enséñame donde tengo que firmar (If that's what we need to do, show me where I need to sign)." And you'd best believe, before I walked across the stage to accept my degree, my father had paid the loan off in full. I recognize what a privilege it was to have parents who were able to support me both emotionally and financially—and also that that privilege most likely came with sacrifices that, to this day, I don't fully know about.

Growing up in the Bronx, I was almost always surrounded by predominantly Black and Latinx folks. I didn't pay attention to my racial and ethnic identity until I went to college—the first time I was surrounded by a majority of white people. This was an adjustment, to say the least. Because of my limited interactions with white folks, many of my perceptions about them were influenced by what I saw on television. I did not know what to expect when I arrived at my college dorm and met my three white roommates.

I can vividly recall my first interaction with one of them. On move-in day, my roommate pulled me outside, away from our other roommates, to speak with me. I noticed that he was holding something in his hand, then realized it was a Confederate flag.

"Hey, I just wanted to ask, could I put this up?" he asked. "You know, my family is from the South. It is part of our heritage, and I wanted to make sure you were cool with it."

At the time, I didn't really understand the full gravity of the history behind that flag, so I said, "Yeah, you can put that up." It was not until a week later, after gaining a better understanding of what the flag truly meant, that I asked him to take it down. It was an interesting moment for me, because suddenly I had to contend with what it meant to be Black in a space where no one looked like me.

I faced another shock once classes started. I very quickly learned that my New York City public education had failed to prepare me for the rigors of college. But while I had to play catch-up on an academic level, I quickly acclimated to the collegiate lifestyle. I played basketball for three years, winning several awards along the way.

I also found a brotherhood in Alpha Phi Alpha, the first intercollegiate Greek-letter fraternity established for Black men. As a member of this esteemed fraternity, I firmly planted myself in leadership roles and, by my junior year, held leadership positions within our chapter and across the National Pan-Hellenic Council. On Sunday evenings, I cohosted *The Quiet Storm,* a radio show on Brown University's radio station, WBRU. And like many college-aged young men, I dated, eventually meeting the amazing woman I would later marry and have a brilliant and beautiful daughter with.

Providence in the 1990s

I arrived in Providence in 1993 to find a city struggling with poverty, unemployment, poor housing, and crime. Navigating the streets from the dorm to classroom buildings and through other parts of downtown was a heart-quickening experience.

The city recovered a bit in the mid- to late 1990s, riding the coattails of a national economic surge that continued right up until the 2000 stock market correction. Providence (and, really, all of Rhode Island) was usually late to the party of an economic boom and among the first to leave. Nevertheless, Providence underwent a small renaissance of its own. In 1994, the opening of Waterplace Park and the Riverwalk provided a sparkling venue for entertainment open to all.

Changes in the demographics of Providence were dramatic. While the overall population had been declining in 1990, it grew by about 8 percent in the next decade, even as the number of non-Latinx whites declined (Strongin, 2017). The composition of the city's population changed substantially and significantly. By 2000, Latinx residents represented about 30 percent of the population (Vasquez, 2003). Providence has the largest Latinx population in Rhode Island and the second largest in all of New England. Since 2000, the median income for Providence families has increased 20 percent, reversing a decline from 1990 to 2000. However, more than a quarter of the city's population continues to live below the federal poverty level, including more than 35 percent of children.

As the racial and ethnic diversity of the city's population increased, similar changes occurred in the public school system. The number of non-Latinx whites in the school population has declined since 1994, and the overall diversity of the school system has increased. Sadly, however, the number of students below the poverty level has increased dramatically; the city ranks third worst in the nation for childhood poverty (Rhode Island KIDS COUNT, 2020).

A Promise Kept

I graduated from college with dual degrees in business management and marketing. I promised my father when I started college that I would have a job immediately after graduating, so I accepted the first offer I received at a large national rental car company. In this role, I learned about the tenets of customer service and meeting corporate goals and expectations, which ultimately meant upselling to customers. The job emphasized the importance of relationship building and clear communication. However, in this and other early corporate jobs, I never felt encouraged or confident enough to show up with love, care, and vulnerability. In retrospect, these jobs left little room for me to discover what I was passionate about. Although I met some phenomenal people, my early professional experiences never spoke to what I believed to be my greater purpose.

Following my brief time in corporate America, I accepted an offer to join an international child sponsorship and humanitarian nonprofit organization. The offer came about as a result of reconnecting with an older fraternity brother who worked at the organization. He saw something in me that I did not recognize in myself at the time—a penchant for leadership. After all, our fraternity focused on leadership and service to our communities. I quickly began my foray into international humanitarian work. My new role focused on donor sponsorship and major and planned gifts. The organization provided underserved children and families with access to many things that we take for granted, including clean and safe drinking water, safely constructed homes, and schools. They also promoted campaigns against female genital

mutilation, anti–human trafficking initiatives, small-business incuba-
tors, and so much more. This work afforded me the opportunity to
travel the world and see firsthand the importance of humanitarian
efforts and the positive impact they have on individual lives. I had
found *soul work*—work that was greater than myself. I came to realize
that despite the challenges I encountered as a young man, I was living
and beginning to thrive in an economically developed world and, com-
paratively speaking, had a fair amount of privilege.

In the four years I spent working for Plan International USA (for-
merly Childreach), I started to notice a pattern among the families in
the various countries I visited. Regardless of socioeconomic circumstance, the parents almost always had a deep commitment to the
education of their children. While many of the parents themselves had
been unable to complete formal education, they considered it imperative that their own children engage in schooling. I realized that access
to education improves socioeconomic prospects not only directly for
students but for generations to come.

The late Nobel prize–winning economist Amartya Sen asserted
that access to education is essential in gaining access to other rights,
as it determines human freedoms and what people can achieve in their
lives (Walker, 2005). In the absence of these freedoms, individuals
often remain subject to limited circumstances (Sen, 2011). It took leaving the United States for me to see that the people I encountered in the
developing world were not so different from those in my hometown of
the Bronx, where parents also realize the importance of education in
enabling upward mobility for their children.

Discovering The Met and Big Picture Learning

As my work at the international level seemed to be reaching a pla-
teau, I felt it was time to come home and build on the foundation I'd
first established in Providence. I knew I wanted to work with children and in education, but entering the teaching profession was the
furthest thing from my mind. Teaching was not even a part of what

I believed to be my purpose or my life's trajectory. Upon my return to the United States, I reconnected with Danique Dolly, a dear friend from my college days. We were both sons of New York City: I attended New York City public high schools, while Danique attended Fordham Preparatory School, a private school located on Fordham University's campus. (My impression of the Fordham University campus, a mere stone's throw from my bedroom window, was of a gilded cage; I felt that the walls had been constructed to keep out people like me.)

Danique originally crossed my path while I was completing my undergraduate studies and he was completing his master's degree in teaching at Brown University. As members of different fraternities, we participated in several projects around Providence working with young people. He saw how I interacted with them and, as he often did, challenged my decision to be a business major. "We need more brothers in education," he would say. He would tell me I could make a real difference. I brushed it off at the time because I thought, *As a private school graduate, what does he know about the struggle?* I assumed that because he attended parochial and private schools, he had no clue about the challenges young people faced in the community. I was wrong. Danique's story is a powerful and beautiful one that I hope he will share widely someday.

Running into Danique after so many years was fortuitous, even if I did not see it at the time. He told me that he was teaching at an innovative school in Providence: The Metropolitan Regional Career and Technical Center (affectionately known as The Met). The Met was Big Picture Learning's founding school and where the Big Picture Learning design principles of relationships, relevance, and rigor were established. He excitedly shared that the school was a prototype and that similar schools were about to emerge all over the country. We exchanged information and went our separate ways. He subsequently called repeatedly inviting me to visit The Met; he was just as persistent as he had been in college. And I am forever grateful that he was.

When I finally did visit, I witnessed firsthand how this innovative high school was turning the schooling experience into something

I could not have imagined. What I observed were authentic relationships between adults and young people that were grounded in love. Conversations between teachers and students, between teachers and teachers, and between teachers and principals were open and honest, free of hierarchy and judgment, and focused on understanding, empowerment, and responsibility. These were people who cared more about working with young people than working the curriculum, and I thought what they were doing was extraordinary. At this point in my journey, my approach to leading with love, care, and vulnerability—*Leadership Soul,* which I will expound on in the next chapter—was far from developed, but my instincts told me that The Met was a place where I could learn and forge my stance not only as an educator but also as a leader.

Students at The Met are handed the reins of their learning experiences and are empowered to chart their trajectories. What's more, their learning is experiential: they explore powerful, real-world learning experiences through internships. I noticed how comfortable these students were in their interactions and communications with adults, whether they were familiar or not. To say I was impressed would be an understatement.

The Met was the creation of two educators, Dennis Littky and Elliot Washor, who came to Providence in the early 1990s to work with Ted Sizer at Brown University. Sizer was a nationally recognized leader of educational reform in the 1980s and 1990s. In 1984, he founded the Coalition of Essential Schools, a national high school transformation initiative described in *Horace's Compromise* (Sizer, 2004), a book challenging many elements of traditional high schools. Recognizing that school wasn't working for many young people, Littky and Washor challenged one another to reimagine learning experiences without regard to what most schools looked like at the time. The result was The Met, and over the last 25 years, more than 100 Big Picture Learning schools in the United States and another 100-plus around the world have formed to empower young people to create happy, successful lives of their own design.

While thoroughly impressed and excited about what I saw at The Met, I wasn't certain I could see myself in a school setting, and especially not in a classroom. To be quite honest, I'd never previously had the desire to become an educator. Growing up, Black male teachers were few and far between. None of my K–12 teachers or college professors had inspired me to want to pursue education as a possible career.

But perhaps the lack of male teachers of color had an unintended effect. Could it be that the absence of teachers I could relate to or who looked like me made me believe that the classroom was no place for an Afro-Latino man? Did students who looked like me, were raised the same way, and had similar life trajectories *need* an educator like me?

The reality is that the teaching force in the United States is overwhelmingly made up of white women. However, research confirms that teachers of color are "uniquely positioned to improve the performance of students [of color . . . by] directly or indirectly serving as role models, mentors, advocates, or cultural translators" (Egalite et al., 2015, p. 44). There continues to be a real and significant shortage of teachers of color, and in particular male teachers of color, at a time when students of color need them most. Thankfully, campaigns such as Real Men Teach and organizations like the Center for Black Educator Development have been on the rise in recent years, working to recruit and retain male teachers of color.

My introduction to The Met lit a spark in me. I felt that I'd been led to my purpose. I wanted to work with young people in ways that were transformative rather than transactional. I saw my role at The Met as not only making an impact in the lives of others but forever changing my own life as well.

How Teaching Taught Me How to Teach

In 2002, I began my first job as an educator. I became the advisor to a group of young people—Aisha, Arthur, Ashley, Brandon, Chris, Cherolyn, Engers, Joseph, Josue, Jessica, Le'Quise, Manny, Marieli,

Micah, Odyssey, Priscilla, Rachel, and Shawn—who changed my life in many ways. Together, we began our collective and individual journeys at The Met, then in its seventh year.

While entering the classroom was certainly a big transition for me, I felt well supported by The Met and Big Picture Learning culture. I received positive feedback from my peers, who saw my leadership potential. One of my strengths was my "calming," unflappable demeanor, which made it easy for me to work with young people. But I also attempted to bring kindness, honesty, firmness, and a commitment to continuous improvement. I had to own up to things that I did not know about myself and ask for help when I needed it. For me, the most effective way of learning how to support my students was through collaboration.

These 17 young people were my motivation. We grew and evolved together. Over the course of four years, I watched them mature, getting to know their families and their cultures, and on a deeper level, their hearts and minds. Learning alongside them while supporting them as they found their love for learning remains one of the most rewarding experiences of my career and life.

The highly personalized Big Picture Learning approach requires you to lead and learn, meaning that each student or advisee creates and receives detailed attention to their specific learning needs. This is why I know as much as I do about the circulatory system, systolic and diastolic pressures and hypertension, the culinary arts, clothing design, music production, midwifery, trans fats, early childhood and adolescent learning, computer science, architecture, computer-aided design, national abuse laws, forensics, retinopathy of prematurity, playwriting, and marine biology. These were just some of the interests my students had—and areas where they delved deeply to enhance their own learning. To support them in that learning, I needed to delve deep as well. Once students began exploring their interests, their excitement and desire to learn more was limitless, and I found myself matching them in their excitement as we embarked on their learning journeys together. Until they joined The Met, most of these young people had found school boring and irrelevant. As we worked to cocreate and codesign their learning experiences, one of our mutually agreed-upon goals was to ensure that their time at The Met was anything but boring.

Beginning my teaching career at a Big Picture Learning school like The Met was really the only entry point into the field of education that made sense for me. I had never wanted to replicate the learning environments that I experienced growing up; I wanted more for the next generation of learners. The late bell hooks (1994) profoundly asserted that education in its purest form is a "practice of freedom"—a form of teaching and learning that is engaging and exciting for both teachers and learners. In this "practice of freedom," both parties equally contribute to and share in the learning experience. Students are not just taught information that they are expected to commit to memory and recall when asked; they are also taught to think critically in a nonconformist, unconfined way. Adults who educate as a "practice of freedom" teach "not merely to share information but to share in the intellectual and spiritual growth of our babies" (hooks, 1994, p. 13).

When students are taught in this liberatory manner, the lessons they learn carry over into their lives outside the classroom—an everpresent reminder that we are all born with an insatiable thirst to learn and grow. We are born curious, and we are excited when we discover new things. Yet somehow the way in which learning is presented makes it uncool, unexciting, and straight-up boring, often as early as grade school.

What I found at The Met was an organization and culture predicated on love, care, and vulnerability. All facets of the school—students, teachers, and administration—were guided by these principles. I felt comfortable at The Met even as I was still learning my craft. In working with students who had continuously been kept from quality, loving opportunities and while navigating through challenging circumstances, my fellow teachers had my back and would not let me fail. I often reflect on how much I learned about love, care, and vulnerability from and with and for my colleagues. The relationships I forged at The Met stay with me even now.

My Leadership Responsibility Journey

In my first roles as an advisor (2002–2006) and then principal (2006–2009), my Leadership Soul emerged. I learned that, as a leader, it is important that I adapt to whatever a situation, moment, or movement requires. And while I personally find leading from the front to be my least favorite type of leadership, I embrace it when necessary. My preference is to lead from the side, to support others along their own leadership development journey. Oftentimes, educators who have worked relentlessly in support of their students position themselves as the lone experts rather than elevating and holding up students and their accomplishments, but I find that this practice can be isolating and counterproductive.

Following my experience at The Met, I moved to the company behind the school, Big Picture Learning, where I've held several positions: director of school reform and innovation (2010–2012), national director of schools (2012–2015), and co–executive director (2015–present). Following four years with my advisory and four more as an administrator at The Met, over the subsequent decade my work shifted to focus on expanding the Big Picture Learning approach beyond Providence. I accepted the opportunity to head up expansion efforts in and around Newark, New Jersey, which, at the time, was going through its own educational transformation. The transition from principal and assistant district director made sense for me at the time for a number of reasons. First, it was time for me to return to the New York City area to be closer to my family. Second, I was seeking professional advancement and wanted to apply what I'd learned from my previous roles to creating more systemic change, including by advising the mayor of Newark's team regarding matters of education. And third, I wanted to help grow Big Picture Learning schools in Newark and throughout New Jersey.

Though still part of the Big Picture Learning national organization, I found myself working independently for the first time. Sure, I still benefited from working closely with Elliot and learning alongside him. But I didn't have a physical office to go into every day, so I needed to develop discipline to work alone. I had to do a lot of preparatory work in advance of meetings to understand the city's rich history and the plethora of nuanced alliances and relationships that existed among the city's key decision makers.

In most cases, I had neither formal authority nor control; I was merely an intermediary. I could only effect change in practice and pedagogy up to a certain point. I had to learn how to be a beneficial partner in a large school district. There were times I had to shift and pivot, such as when a new leadership team unceremoniously shut down a multiyear school startup project that I had been asked to initiate. Yet I was also able to be directly involved in systems-level change in a high-profile district heavily influenced by outside philanthropy. I learned that alliances can, if cultivated appropriately, be leveraged later. Many of the folks I connected with in Newark continue to be collaborative partners on a national level to this day.

I was invited to take on the role of national director of schools in 2012. The position allowed me to apply skills I had honed at a regional level—relationship building chief among them—and applied them to expanding Big Picture Learning—not just by starting new schools but also by helping existing schools in our burgeoning network continue to refine their practices to benefit students, families, and communities across the country.

Over my time at The Met and then in Newark, I built relationships with principals across the country and periodically facilitated coaching and development with select schools in the network. As in my previous roles, my leadership was embraced by former colleagues in truly powerful ways. I had the backing of my predecessor, Kari Thierer, who was kind and supportive in my transition, allowing me to reach out to her for advice and periodically check in as I settled into the role. I still interacted with district leaders and philanthropic organizations, but now I was equipped with a more specific understanding of the challenges and opportunities they identified as they worked within their districts to launch new innovative schools.

Early on, Big Picture Learning founders Dennis Littky and Elliot Washor committed to hiring and elevating people from the communities they were serving. This was as true at the executive director level as it was at the advisor level. Dennis and Elliot were among my primary supporters, and they prepared me to take on various leadership roles as time went on.

I learned a lot through trial and error when I first became co–executive director, but I am fortunate to have entered into this role with longtime friend and colleague Andrew Frishman, a fellow advisor at The Met, who is one of the brightest and most thoughtful leaders I've had the pleasure of working alongside. The transition was also facilitated by a tremendous board of directors who understood the importance and complexity of a successful succession.

On a personal level, the executive director role requires an amount of travel that forced me—for the first time—to take a hard look at work-life balance. I took on the responsibility of coordinating and establishing the growth of our national programmatic team by conceptualizing and launching our regional structure, which included the addition of regional directors, many of whom later ascended to the national leadership team.

So far in my professional career, I have been blessed by working with remarkable individuals who, without ever thinking about it, embrace Leadership Soul and infuse love, care, and vulnerability into their relationships. The Met and Big Picture Learning powerfully embody Leadership Soul throughout a school's design and operation.

Sharing My Leadership Journey

Most of what I know about leadership—its purpose, principles, and practices—I learned from my parents, my family, and close connections in our community. Again and again throughout my career, I have relearned what they taught me. My focus on love, care, and vulnerability, forged in childhood, has formed the foundation of my own leadership with and through others, particularly the young people I have had the privilege to know and serve.

In this book, I share my leadership and teaching experiences with three young men: Josue, Angel, and Shawn. These young men left indelible marks on my leadership journey. I experienced many of my firsts with them, and they helped me learn how to truly teach, lead, and serve. Letters written to these former students and their family members form the centerpiece of my narrative; for me, sharing them is the ultimate act of vulnerability. As with the letter to my younger self at the start of this book, these letters offer me the opportunity to share thoughts I couldn't express at the time because I didn't have the experience, language, foresight or, in some cases, courage to do so.

Why These Stories?

In Ghana, the Akan people have a word in the Twi language—*sankofa*—that literally means "to go back and get it." The term refers to bringing forward what is at risk of being left behind. Implicit to the concept of sankofa is the idea that the past is a guide to the future. I could not leave the memory of Josue, Angel, and Shawn behind. I wanted to write a book to honor them. Their stories have remained with me, and I often find myself thinking about their experiences and our relationships. Although they are no longer with us, they were all uniquely talented, compassionate, brilliant, sharp, and tremendous human beings. Through their stories, I hope to draw out what I have learned from knowing them and working with them and reflect on the passions that they possessed.

My goal as an education leader has been constant: to lift up and center the best interests of the young people we serve. When I began teaching at The Met, I hoped that my presence would make a positive impact on the education experiences of my students. I soon realized that these young people would in turn have a tremendous impact on my own learning and development as an educator, leader, and parent.

Welcome to *Leadership Soul.*

2 | Why This Book?

Teaching is a performative act. And it is that aspect of our work that offers the space for change, invention, spontaneous shifts, that can serve as a catalyst drawing out the unique elements in each classroom.

—bell hooks

Over the last 10 years, I have been intensely curious about leaders and leadership, particularly (but not exclusively) in education. Today, many books and articles challenge leaders to recognize the limitations of older, more conventional leadership archetypes that require one person to be the holder of all knowledge. But few of these works are written by men of color. As a Black man—specifically, Afro-Caribbean and Afro-Latino—I have had both the privilege of seeing myself in many of the young people I have worked with and the disadvantage of seeing and experiencing firsthand the damage that is done when marginalized students are alienated from their own learning processes. (I note here that while this book prioritizes the experiences of Black and Brown young men, I do recognize and salute the significance and importance of work focused on Black and Brown women.)

In my explorations, I have been especially intrigued by leaders who address or wish to address issues of equity and inclusion. What kind of leadership and leaders are needed? What kind of leadership and leaders do we have? To what kind of leadership do our leaders aspire? I choose to lean into vulnerability and make myself accessible to those I serve, and I wanted to share my story so that others may see why I embrace this form of leadership. I write this book with full transparency. My journey through leadership has had ups and downs, and I continue to learn from my experiences.

Multiple forces are currently converging to signal a sea change in how our society prepares young people for success in their work, personal, and civic lives. The lockdown and isolation mandates due to COVID-19 created cascading shocks to the education system, leading to plummeting engagement and attendance levels that have yet to return to full prepandemic rates. Black and Latinx students still graduate at rates significantly lower than their white peers and have less access to deep and productive learning experiences that prepare them for postsecondary success. Schools are in crisis, unable or unwilling to serve all their students well, and this is particularly the case with respect to marginalized students. This crisis extends beyond the traditional school curriculum to physical and mental health and well-being: schools desperately need help addressing students' overall development.

The statistics can be alarming:

- More than 1.2 million students drop out of high school in the United States alone each year, which works out to a loss of 7,000 students a day (DoSomething.org, 2023).
- Approximately one-quarter of high school freshmen do not graduate from high school within four years (DoSomething.org, 2023).
- Colleges are also seeing significant dropout rates. The percentage of college students who do not graduate within six years is 57 percent for public institutions, with 24 percent remaining enrolled either full- or part-time, and 33 percent dropping out entirely (P, 2020).

The waste of talent and energy is appalling. We can only guess at the larger number of students who do not drop out but languish in their seats, obtaining a high school or college degree but remaining wholly unprepared to navigate an increasingly challenging workforce and economy. This is happening at a time of growing recognition that education is an essential means of obtaining and securing individual and community prosperity. We are at risk of wasting an enormous talent pool of future professionals, passionate tradespersons, and talented craftspeople who could make outsized contributions to our society and economy even as they ensure their own economic security and personal and professional fulfillment.

Our public education system fails to engage students in learning experiences that meet their unique interests, strengths, learning styles, and contexts. It fails to offer opportunities for students to truly explore career aspirations. It fails to develop the 21st century skills and social capital students need to fulfill their potential. In other words, the system fails to personalize learning in the ways that are most relevant to building competence and supporting aspiration. Further, schools often aggressively deny many students access to learning opportunities and learning environments that will prepare them for personal and professional success.

Current and conventional leadership approaches do not appear to be up to these challenges. The most marginalized students—students of color, students with low income, students with learning differences, and English language learners—are often viewed through a deficit lens, with each group depicted as a monolith. Educators assume that these students lack the knowledge or cultural capital to succeed, according to dominant definitions of academic success (Yosso, 2005). *The myth of meritocracy suggests that anyone who works hard enough can realize their greatest potential regardless of socioeconomic hurdles.* Lani Guinier (2016) challenges this myth, foundational to inequity, in her book *The Tyranny of the Meritocracy.*

It is imperative that we see young people as individuals while also understanding the systemic factors that contribute to their marginalization. I have chosen to focus in this book on Black and Latino males and their intersecting identities, which are not limited to race and gender. Khalifa and colleagues (2016) refer to these students as "individuals from racially oppressed communities that have been marginalized—both legally and discursively—because of their non-dominant race, ethnicity, religion, language, or citizenship" (p. 1275). Their marginalization is often compounded by the intersection of membership in more than one of these categories.

Marginalization exists in almost every aspect of the lives of these Black and Brown youths, but I have seen it play out most pathologically in schools, where students are labeled, grouped, and tracked into academic and career pathways with limited access to resources, including caring and competent teachers. Such marginalization comes in part from insidious policies and practices that deny these young people access to the kinds of educational opportunities and learning environments that we know are essential for their success and well-being.

The American public education system has historically, systematically, and inequitably favored white middle- and upper-income students, normalizing and centering their experiences to the detriment of others. Despite what is often hailed as transformational, the 1954 *Brown v. Board of Education* decision did not end segregation of our public school system. In fact, in the greater New York City area the schools are just as segregated as they were prior to that ruling. And, in far too many communities across this country, our schools remain segregated and inherently unequal, with many schools often further divided by language (Orfield et al., 2012). But Black and Latino male students are so much more than a catalog of their deficits, with abundant and varied assets that remain largely untapped by schools.

Playing Catch-Up

Black and Latino boys are frequently grouped in research literature because their schooling experiences are often quite similar. For example, Black and Latinx students are more likely to face harsher punitive measures than white students for the same transgressions, regardless of how minor those infringements may be. However, Noguera and colleagues (2012) caution against grouping Black and Latino males together, asserting that the lack of research on the experiences of Latino boys and men exclusively is problematic. "Most of the studies available have focused on Black men exclusively or have aggregated both groups in ways that render the experiences of Latino men less visible than those of Blacks," they write. "In those studies, Latino men are not given the same focus as African American men, minimizing the diversity of experiences among men of color" (p. 5).

According to the National Institute for Early Education Research, Black preschoolers are least likely than other groups to receive high-quality early education, a known predictor of further education gains (Friedman-Krauss et al., 2022). Even before entering kindergarten, Black children (and especially Black boys) are subjected to inordinately high rates of discipline. Once enrolled in school, Black and Latino boys have the lowest conventional academic outcomes of all. They are also typically excluded from gifted and talented programs and overrepresented in special education classes (Wright & Ford, 2019).

No doubt these issues have a direct connection to how these boys and young men fare as they grow. The Schott Foundation for Public Education (2015) found that during the 2012–2013 academic year, the national graduation rate for Black males was 59 percent, compared to 65 percent for Latino males and 80 percent for white males. As Fergus (2010) writes, "Black boys are more likely than any other group to be suspended and expelled from school, and they are more likely to be arrested in a school setting" (p. 20). Both Black and Latino males are stigmatized in our culture, but Black men especially are depicted either as criminals or as an endangered species. School and classroom practices often "adultify" young Black and Latino males, stripping them of their innocence to allow more punitive actions to be taken against them for discipline issues.

Wanted: The Leadership of Uncommon Leaders

Historically, Black leaders in education have steered the ship of their communities. In fact, throughout U.S. history, Black educational leaders have been at the vanguard of the struggle against inequality. Black and

Brown educational leadership is a radical act heavily tied to resistance against the status quo. Categorizing it as a type of protest leadership focused on equality not just for Black and Brown learners but for all learners, Dantley (2009) writes that "African American leadership is not limited to organizational management but pursues the radical reconstructions of society" (p. 43). In the profound words of Murtadha and Watts (2005), "a major purpose of leadership is to create worlds of difference and the reconstruction of reality" (p. 591). At the core of being a Black leader is this notion of resistance against systems that would have us believe the communities we are serving—those who look like us—are not capable or deserving of an emancipatory education.

Literature that centers the experiences and narratives of Black and Brown male educators is scarce. In the absence of these stories, assumptions about how we lead are often misinformed. "Unfortunately, the omission of Black leadership narratives, along with an [in]adequate analysis of the contexts in which leadership has worked, limits our ability to develop ways to improve schools and communities for children who live in poverty and children of color who are becoming the majority in this nation's schools," write Murtadha and Watts (2005, p. 591). Anderson (1990) observes that Blackness in educational administration processes, as in other facets of schooling, is rendered virtually invisible.

Today, leadership is being challenged as never before. In nearly every aspect of society, leadership is failing us. There is a lack of trust, of competence, of authenticity. We need uncommon leaders who center love, care, and vulnerability—leadership centered on one's soul.

What Is Leadership Soul?

Leadership Soul challenges and disrupts traditional approaches to teaching and leading Black and Latinx youth, who have been scrutinized and pathologized, their capabilities denigrated and their cultures both dismissed and blamed for any achievement gaps. Education reform efforts have only exacerbated these persistent inequalities by advocating policies and practices that ignore structural barriers like racism, segregation, and poverty. Too many currently celebrated ideologies and practices suggest that attitude adjustments, self-control, grit, and bootstrapping are the foundations for success. These out-of-touch pedagogical approaches alienate Black and Brown students and diminish the invaluable role of informal learning experiences.

Leadership Soul is built on three pillars: love, care, and vulnerability. In the context of education, *love* is a deep commitment to educating learners in a way that seeks their empowerment and upliftment. Author and activist bell hooks (1994) refers to love as a radical act, and Larson and Murtadha (2005) center love in leadership, acknowledging that in order to educate, we must love those whom we lead. *Care* means approaching education with the understanding that certain injustices affect specific groups of learners in unique ways and assuming responsibility for dismantling these inequalities. *Vulnerability* is an educator's willingness to bring their authentic self to those they lead, sharing their own experiences to create deeper bonds with their students and colleagues.

Love Is Embracing

Love is the soil in which caring and vulnerability are nourished. I challenge leaders and educators to cast aside the conventional understanding of love. The love I pursue is an emancipatory and self-determining force aligned to the Black feminist conceptualization of love. This is not romantic love; rather, it is a force that channels liberatory power (Banda et al., 2020). This type of love embraces the community and champions the emancipation of the community from the power structures and oppressive forms of leadership that inflict and reinforce inequalities. In this book, I make the case that effective leaders and educators must love their learners, care for them, and be vulnerable in their relationships with them. The love I speak of throughout this book transforms caring and vulnerability and is at the heart of my Leadership Soul.

I have experienced this empowering love in my relationships with my students. It was infused in my deep conversations with them, not only about the learning we were experiencing together but also about the bond we were forming through truth and honesty. I brought this love to my relationships with my students' family members as well, being open to their concerns about their children's learning and development and even my teaching, which I always strove to improve. Fortunately, I was a teacher and then a principal at The Met, where relationships grounded in such love could flourish and where openness and honesty allowed my Leadership Soul to develop and contribute to our students' success.

Care Is Service

Caring is helping—humbly and without reservation. Leaders with soul bring highly individualized caring to learners and serve families and the community. Such caring therefore takes on community and cultural components. Within Black and Latinx communities, care often incorporates an obligation that extends beyond self.

Caring without a foundation of love is not the Leadership Soul I want leaders to exhibit. Caring without love is intellectual and technical, bounded and constrained. Banda and colleagues (2020) discuss what it means to conceptualize and practice care as a collective and communal responsibility rather than "formulaic and institutionalized requirements" (p. 3).

I have sought to express my caring *about* and my caring *for* my students through my deeply personal learning relationship with each individual I've had the privilege to teach, mentor, or lead. After all, "one student at a time" is the motto of all Big Picture Learning schools. When I began my work with Big Picture Learning, I quickly recognized it as an organization where my Leadership Soul could flourish and I could create my own leadership signature based on love, care, and vulnerability.

Vulnerability Is Openness

Vulnerability guided by love dismantles the barriers between leaders and those they serve. Love stimulates an openness to being changed, to learning with, through, and for others. I always strove to be radically open with my students and their families, making my teaching practices open to their review and encouraging their openness as well. Sharing my aspirations, my fears, and my joys with them lowered the walls and encouraged them to share with me, too.

Too often, traditional approaches view marginalized learners through a deficit lens, pathologizing their learning and schooling by focusing solely on individual behaviors as opposed to structural barriers (Ginwright, 2006). Banda and colleagues (2020) observe that love, care, and vulnerability are often messy and painful for people of color, given the multiple forms of oppression they face. Leaders must therefore assess their ability to love, care, and be vulnerable. These elements must be at the center of how educators approach learners as we guide them through the foundational phases of their lives.

Critical Versus Conventional Education

Leading from the soul—exhibiting love, care, and vulnerability—is different from being guided by the mind. There will, of course, always be a need for attention to the technical aspects of leadership—organizational and cultural change management, strategic and analytical thinking, budgeting and behavior management. But, as important as these are, they are not enough to address the challenges of leading Black and Brown youth who continue to be kept on the margins.

Educational leaders must work for social justice if they wish to do more than tackle existing inequities. Black and Latinx educators occupy unique positions in that they play dual roles as both leaders and members of a minoritized group. "Because minoritized students have been disadvantaged by historically oppressive structures, and because educators and schools have been—intentionally or unintentionally—complicit in reproducing this oppression, culturally responsive school leaders have a principled, moral responsibility to counter this oppression," write Khalifa and colleagues (2016, p. 1275). Critical education theorist Paulo Freire considered education to be a tool for liberation, especially for the most marginalized of society. His approach centered the lived experiences of oppressed groups and idealized education "as a transformative, context-laden, grassroots political movement" (Miller et al., 2011, p. 1083) that has the potential to promote social justice.

Conventional educational leadership emphasizes the reinforcement of protocols, assessment, and instruction while ignoring the needs of marginalized students. Absence of compassion and understanding too often serves to reinforce and extend oppression. Early-career educators may be asking what they can do to meet the requirements of their school while combating unequal systems and practices. In part, the answer is to act with intentionality—be purposeful in the spaces that you occupy.

Leadership Soul focuses on three young men and their experiences as a way to explore a leadership framework of love, care, and vulnerability. Such a framework should be implemented with all students, but especially with those who are commonly mischaracterized with a deficit narrative. Young women require similar nurturing, but I focus on these three young men—my former students—because their lived experiences mirrored my own. They needed more attention and more support, just as I did. The low expectations that the world had for them as young Black and Latino men cast an ominous shadow of doubt and bred a fear of self-fulfilling prophecies.

It is imperative that we change the way we see our students and their realities. This requires fundamental changes in how we lead. I caution education leaders against perpetuating the damaging narrative that Black and Latinx learners are in crisis, because it may give the false impression that Black and Latinx learners have, for whatever reason, simply found themselves on the wrong side of an achievement gap. Meaningful and effective leadership must acknowledge that the cascading intergenerational effects of systemic racism are at the core of the issues facing Black and Latinx learners and their communities. It is incumbent on us to transform the structures of education systems in response.

While we are obligated to actively push back against practices that are not rooted in social justice, Professor Bettina L. Love (2019) reminds teachers that they are not themselves responsible for dismantling a flawed education system. "As educators," she writes, "we must accept that schools are places of Whiteness, White rage, and disempowerment. We cannot fall into narratives of racial progress that romanticize 'how far we've come' or suggest that success comes from Blacks being more like Whites" (p. 40). Love calls on educational leaders to name the injustices that exist within schooling and adopt teaching practices that root out and reject those injustices.

Khalifa and colleagues (2016) write:

> Culturally responsive school leaders are responsible for promoting a school climate inclusive of minoritized students, particularly those marginalized within most school contexts. Such leaders also maintain a presence in, and relationships with, community members they serve. They lead professional developments to ensure their teachers and staff, and the curriculum, are continuously responsive to minoritized students. (p. 1274)

Working in the education system requires a great deal of commitment. Effective educators must be able to connect with their students in ways that support their indignation toward the inequities that they and their students regularly face. Professor and researcher Jeff Duncan-Andrade (2009) exhorts educators to examine the lived experiences of their students as connected to their lives outside the schoolhouse. Young people need to know that their teachers and administrators see their humanity and advocate for them through actionable and teachable examples. "Educators who foster this type of solidarity with and among students recognize the distinction between being liked and being loved by their students," writes Duncan-Andrade. "Being liked comes from avoiding unpleasant situations, whereas being loved is often painful" (p. 188). Leaders must occupy spaces that use whatever resources are available to address issues in their students' lives. Recognizing that these resources and opportunities may not be possible in all school models is one of the reasons Big Picture Learning exists.

I do not believe I could have had the same impact in education had I entered the field through a conventional public school. I wanted to serve Black and Brown youth beyond providing quality leadership and instruction—I wanted to ensure that they were viewed as humans. After all, these young people with tremendous potential enter our schools with gifts, talents, and abilities that need to be nurtured and cultivated. It was not until I learned about The Met and Big Picture Learning that I realized a public school existed that did these very things; the protection of young people's capabilities and hearts was something that I had only ever heard about happening in private and independent schools. Had I taught at a more conventional school, I find it hard to believe that I would have had the same impact or experiences as I did at The Met. Being allowed the privilege to honor and understand our students is the first step in truly building community. Before our students can experience true personalized learning, we must know their stories. And to build the trust necessary to earn their stories, it is essential that we as teachers and leaders have the courage and conviction to know and share our own histories and stories. The relationships I forged with students and the community we built together created a closeness that often mirrored what they had with their own families. This cannot be done well within the confining structures of a conventional school design.

Each student at The Met is part of a small learning community of students called an *advisory*. That original cohort of 17 young people was my first advisory. Each advisory is supported and led by an advisor, a teacher or other staff member who works closely with the group and forms personal relationships with each advisee, their families, and their mentors at the students' internship sites. The advisors are charged with fully supporting each young person, both academically and socioemotionally, throughout their four years at the school.

Advisories typically range from 15 to 25 students, and in most Big Picture Learning schools, advisors remain with the same advisory group for all four years, from 9th through 12th grade.

Placing students at the center of their learning truly engages and challenges them and makes learning authentic and relevant. Each student participates in a series of interest-driven internships where they work closely with mentors, learning in real-world workplaces. Parents and families are actively involved in the learning process, helping to shape each student's learning plan and serving as resources to the school community. Mentoring, an important part of leading through love, care, and vulnerability, is embedded in the advisory model. The result is a student-centered learning design in which students are actively invested in their learning and challenged to pursue their interests by a supportive community of educators, professionals, and family members.

Other design elements of The Met that give evidence of attention to love, care, and vulnerability include the following:

- **Paying attention to the whole student.** Each Big Picture Learning school starts with this premise, focusing on students' interests, passions, experiences, challenges, community, and family. Knowing these things about young people gives us unique insight into working with them and offers entry points to connect them to resources to support their physical and mental health.

- **Focusing on students' strengths, not their weaknesses.** Too often, educators or other adult professionals enter schools and methodically diagnose what is wrong with students. What are their gaps in learning? Where should improvement efforts be focused? Instead of focusing on students' so-called deficits, The Met focuses on their strengths. Over time, we find that learning gaps are resolved as part of this process, or at least become so diminished in comparison to the students' strengths that they become insignificant. All of us have deficits—things we don't do incredibly well. But we all also have individual strengths that position those deficits as secondary. We play to our own strengths, and as educators, we should play to students'.

- **Encouraging students to "leave to learn."** One of the key distinguishing elements of the Big Picture Learning approach employed at The Met is to work with students in ways that elucidate their interests. As I mentioned earlier, my own advisees had an expansive and eclectic set of interests that ranged far beyond my areas of expertise. So where in the world can students possibly learn about *all* of their areas of interest? The answer is in the question—they can learn in the world beyond the walls of the school. When students leave school to learn in their community through internships and mentorships, they're able to explore potential career interests, learn practical skills, and develop long-lasting relationships that are invaluable in opening up a wider range of options for the future.

- **Allowing students to demonstrate their learning in a wide variety of ways.** Whether it's through presentations of learning, exhibitions, student-led conferences, or more traditional practices, The Met offers students a diverse selection of rigorous assessment methods to demonstrate their grasp of content and its application.

The Met was the perfect place to develop and shape my Leadership Soul. My focus on love, care, and vulnerability began with my first cohort of students and expanded as I took on new leadership roles. Along the way, I found that once you start developing your Leadership Soul, you apply those kinds of thinking, learning, and performing to all the relationships you create.

Continuing the Journey

Now that you've been introduced to the concept of Leadership Soul, we can take a closer look at how leading with love, care, and vulnerability can be practiced in the real world—and how sometimes it's still a work in progress. Chapter 3 explores Leadership Soul in greater detail and introduces the Big Picture Learning approach, showing how this innovative school design can best serve learners who have been inadequately served by far too many conventional schools.

In Chapter 4, you'll meet Josue, an enigmatic and complex young man who would most likely have been stereotyped and pigeonholed in a traditional school setting. His penchant for jokes and harmless mischief would have undoubtedly placed him in detention or out-of-school suspension. This chapter focuses on how educational leaders can recognize and foster love through leadership in a meaningful way. It also reflects on how Josue could have been better served by his postsecondary education as a first-generation college student.

Chapter 5 introduces Angel, a talented young man and natural leader with hopes of becoming an architect. His tenacity and drive were evident in his desire to provide for and support his family, which at times may have been overshadowed by his hubris. You will learn about the importance of care and what that meant for this young man struggling to find stability in his life. A precarious home situation meant that his school served as a steady fixture in his life—until his ultimate dismissal. As you reflect on Angel's story, I challenge you to think about how student discipline relates to educating the whole child.

Chapter 6 focuses on Shawn, a kind and insightful young man. He was an avid reader with limitless curiosity. He took advantage of every opportunity to build things, literally with his hands and figuratively by creating bonds between his classmates and community, revealing his natural diplomatic abilities. Shawn was the type of learner who exhibited sensitivity, compassion, and a willingness to support others, often at great cost to his own well-being. This chapter addresses how vulnerability in educational leadership should include humility and exclude the notions of superiority and supremacy that so often dominate in-school settings.

In Chapter 7, I reflect on what leaders I know have accomplished while on their quest to develop their Leadership Soul, and how other leaders might apply this style of leadership to their own journeys. I also describe and reflect upon significant actions that make a difference for marginalized youth.

The Conclusion recaps the steps on the journey to developing Leadership Soul based on love, care, and vulnerability, and offers inspiration for you as you take on this effortful but indescribably vital challenge.

Finally, I've written two important letters to young people who are still with us. The first is to Michael Walters, a young man who weathered a great deal to achieve the success that eludes many Black and Brown youth. Michael's story offers hope for Black and Latinx learners; my letter to him communicates a sincere and honest commitment to honor and value his, and his fellow students', greatest abilities. Michael's letter is followed by a letter to my daughter, Bella—the culmination of my Leadership Soul.

The world has changed drastically over the past few years, so much so that the new normal has yet to be identified. I wrote this book while navigating through the ongoing challenges precipitated by the COVID-19 pandemic and heightened awareness and significance of the Black Lives Matter movement. I acknowledge that we cannot go back to the way things were before, because it is clear to careful observers that the old ways were not working. Political and social currents have reached the crisis stage, and America's unequal and inequitable treatment of its disenfranchised must be profoundly improved if we hope to remain sustainable as a society. Our systems and institutions demand more than incremental reformation; they call out for completely new iterations to replace the inadequate and crumbling status quo—none more so than our public education system.

3 | Leading with Love, Care, and Vulnerability

I said to my children, "I'm going to work and do everything that I can do to see that you get a good education. I don't ever want you to forget that there are millions of God's children who will not and cannot get a good education, and I don't want you to feel that you are better than they are. For you will never be what you ought to be until they are what they ought to be."

—Martin Luther King Jr.

Historically, groups of marginalized young people have had stern, harsh, and, at times, militant forms of leadership thrust upon them. There is an assumption that tough love is needed to guide them; anything else shows weakness. Black male educators have often been tasked with the responsibility of acting as disciplinarians, especially for Black boys: "Of the many socially constructed and contested images of Black men that circulate the American cultural landscape, one that continues to resonate with multiple audiences is that of the Black male patriarch who exercises disciplinary authority over Black children," writes Brockenbrough (2015, p. 500). At the same time, several studies highlight leaders who effectively employ culturally relevant methods of teaching that "reflect insider insights into Black culture and culturally rooted modes of care for Black children" (p. 501).

Some adults have a savior complex when it comes to working with students from marginalized populations. But students do not need a benevolent figure to offer lessons of grit and tell them to pull

45

themselves up by the bootstraps. This self-serving approach does not benefit students. Instead, what young people need is someone who aims to understand them and meet them exactly where they are. Throughout my time in education, I have learned just how important the elements of love, care, and vulnerability are—the LCV approach to leadership—not only to my growth and development as a leader but also to the well-being of the young people I serve.

Using LCV as the foundation for leading reshapes both the student learning experience and the cultures, structures, and systems required to provide that experience. An LCV approach redefines the classroom and school by embracing the world outside the school building—the community and the workplace—as the primary learning space. Indeed, many of the most important skills young people can cultivate—such as those related to social-emotional learning, developing workplace competencies, building social capital, and real-world problem solving—are best honed when situated in authentic contexts.

Approach to Leadership

Brené Brown defines a leader as "anyone who takes responsibility for finding the potential in people and processes, and who has the courage to develop that potential" (Brown, 2018, p. 4). Leaders are seldom leaders just because they possess a technical knowledge base. They are leaders because they have the ability to learn deeply and quickly and to apply that learning to the opportunities and challenges faced by their organizations.

In my role as a leader, I find it important to constantly be aware that there is much required and expected of me, but also that I must always learn and grow in my approach to leadership. Admitting that I don't know what I don't know regularly influences how I lead. Too often, male leaders reinforce inequalities by barreling through their work with unfounded machismo. Acknowledging one's limitations and inexperience is central to vulnerable leadership.

Leadership Soul and Critical Theory

The LCV approach to leadership—that is, Leadership Soul—takes a critical approach to education. Critical theory centers social justice and the voices of marginalized groups in pursuit of emancipation, liberation, and equity (Heiser et al., 2017, p. 1). This approach to leadership is unapologetically learner-centered, meaning that what is best for the student is at the core of the work. While this focus may be a challenge in conventional public-school settings that prioritize standards and academic achievement–based accountability metrics, it is vital to ensuring that marginalized students succeed.

Black, Latinx, and other marginalized populations have been mislabeled as "at-risk" learners for far too long (Bass, 2020). Their ability to succeed in life has been compromised by a myopic focus on their academic performance compared with that of white students. The achievement gap presents what Daniels (2012) refers to as a "superior-subordinate measure" that assigns "an inherent level of superiority to white students and a subordinate position to students of color. . . . Black and Brown youth become the focus of deficit discourses" (p. 1). This is merely another way to gloss over persistent inequalities that have yet to be adequately addressed. "The inequitable policies, systems, and structures that predicted the conditions currently witnessed in our schools are rarely part of the conversation," writes Bass (2020). "Reform efforts have not addressed the root cause of the issue, but, rather, tend to chip away at symptoms of the problems" (p. 358). Gloria Ladson-Billings (2006) recommends that we refer to the disparities in academic outcomes and opportunities as "education debt"—the culmination of historical, economic, sociopolitical, and moral elements that shape the realities for these students. To combat this education debt, schools must implement love, care, and vulnerability in ways that deepen learning and build trust with young people.

Leadership Soul is essential to balancing the human and technical aspects of leadership. The core components of love, care, and vulnerability are important individually, but collectively they establish the norms that should guide how we educate young people. These elements are counter to the design of most public schools—far too many of the structures are heavily influenced by the white supremacist culture in which they were created. Too many schools today ignore the lived experiences and culture of anything and anyone not in the majority.

Leadership Through Love

Love-centered leadership is not a new concept (see, for instance, Hoyle & Slater, 2001; Larson & Murtadha, 2002; Miller et al., 2011). That said, love is often an undervalued component of educational leadership. Love creates deep connections with learners and their communities. It establishes a foundation of trust and compassion so that learners know that their well-being is valued.

Larson and Murtadha (2002) assert that "leaders must recognize communities that have been marginalized in our schools and build trusting relationships with them, committing themselves to act out of love rather than fear, and to make decisions based on principles of care, human dignity, love, justice, and equity" (p. 144). With a Leadership Soul approach, this type of love extends to the community to encompass all the intersecting identities of our students. Paolo Freire (1985) advocated for "armed love" in education—a "willingness to forcefully advocate for students, a fierce commitment to teaching and active engagement in the sociopolitical, and often oppressive, processes that shape educational policy" (Rivera-McCutchen, 2019, p. 237). According to Miller and colleagues (2011), "Freire states that leaders who seek change . . . must go to the people humbly, openly, and ready to listen to their ideas" (p. 1082).

This type of love is a tool of resistance and essential to a critical approach to educational leadership. Byrne-Jiménez and Yoon (2019) developed a framework for educational leadership aimed at stemming the tide of rising white supremacy and its impact on marginalized communities and the institutions that serve them. This conceptual framework centers love "because it integrates the personal and the public in service to children" (Byrne-Jiménez & Yoon, 2019, p. 4).

Jackson and colleagues (2014) argue for a specific type of love they call reciprocal love—"an understanding that love for the self is inextricably linked to a love for others" (p. 399). The call for reciprocal love requires us to invest in learners; we must connect ourselves to their successes in ways that both combat structural oppression and improve students' lives. This type of love perhaps predates all others. We see it in the biblical Golden Rule ("Do unto others as you would have others do upon you") and in the even more ancient West African concept of *ubuntu,* which reminds us that we are (and always have been) "what we are because of who we all are."

Leadership Soul takes a radical approach to love. While Freire's concept of armed love is vital to advocating for the most vulnerable learners, I argue that the love that Black female educators often exhibit—one that creates a lasting bond between educator and learner (Jackson et al., 2014; Larson & Murtadha, 2002)—must also be included in the definition. Larson and Murthadha (2002) describe how Black educational leaders are typically underresourced in schools that serve predominantly Black students and families with low income. Yet their approaches to leadership are often embedded in the care shown to their communities and exhibited through an "unwavering belief that all children will experience educational success despite impoverished living conditions and other inhibiting factors" (p. 141). This care is an elegant embrace of Black women's creativity, encompassing beautiful ways to approach the work of leading, building, and educating.

Leadership Through Care

Scholars such as Bass (2020), Delpit (2006), Noddings (1984), and Rivera-McCutchen (2012) suggest that an ethic of care is necessary to help young people succeed in school. Through an ethic of care, educators acknowledge the lived realities of their students and, in turn, lead and teach in ways that combat the problems those students face (Bass, 2020; Noddings, 1984). The theory of care embedded in the Leadership Soul approach aligns with the seminal scholarship on the ethic of care by Nel Noddings (1984, 2002, 2005, 2013). According to Noddings, a strong ethic of care is developed when teachers build relationships with their students based on trust and establish a sense of community (1998, 1992). In the context of Leadership Soul, care must be reciprocal; teachers and students must feel that they both give and receive care (Alder, 2002).

Daniels (2012) argues that Noddings's approach to caring often ignores racial, ethnic, and class issues, as it is grounded in white privilege (p. 8). For a leadership framework to address the specific needs of Black and Brown learners, an ethic of care must also take into account the impact and intersections of race and class.

In framing my approach to leadership, I have examined the ethic of care promoted by Black female educators and Black feminist theories, but ultimately choose to focus on the recently developed Black masculine caring (BMC) framework (Bass, 2012, 2020; Bass & Alston, 2018). Because caring has often been associated with women, male leaders have not often been centered in the dialogue on the subject. Well-established frameworks explain how Black female educators care (Collins, 1989, 2002; Siddle Walker & Snarey, 2004), but until recently, no such framework existed for Black men. Lisa Bass's (2020) BMC framework provides "a language for men who care, specifically Black male school leaders, for whom historical, cultural, and Black masculinity serve to shape the [existing] data" (p. 364). Black masculine caring seeks to dispel stereotype threats by focusing on the capacity of Black men to be caring leaders. When this approach to caring is implemented along with love, new approaches to leadership emerge.

Black masculine caring centers the experiences of Black men and how they negotiate space, place, and their identities. This is of particular importance in the context of teaching and leading because Black men are often working in underresourced schools with high concentrations of Black and Brown learners who live in poverty. These Black male educators are able to bond with Black male students because of similarities in their life experiences, and many of those who practice BMC see themselves as father figures. According to Bass (2020), "The attributes of care expressed by Black male leaders who practice BMC are central to closing achievement and opportunity gaps, as they promote equity, defy color blindness, rebuke meritocracy, and debunk deficit mind-sets and low expectations, while casting down context-neutral mind-sets" (p. 378). What's more, through their positions as leaders, Black men can effectively encourage care for *all* marginalized students, regardless of gender or race.

Leadership Through Vulnerability

There is a commonly held misperception that leaders revealing their vulnerabilities is a sign of weakness, particularly among those who seek strong directive leadership. However, in my experience, the opposite has been true; sharing vulnerability can serve to humanize individual leaders and create conditions for more distributed leadership and collaboration. Vulnerability in education emerges from teaching and learning approaches that are human at the most fundamental level—that is, approaches that accept and understand that teachers and learners are people, not concepts, frameworks, or approaches. Kwenda (2003) introduces the concept of "mutual vulnerability" as a component of cultural justice. He contends that individuals who do not belong to the dominant culture exist in a deficit power-sharing relationship, and that mutual vulnerability can disrupt this imbalance by breaking down the relations of power. As Zinn and colleagues (2009) write, "power encourages stereotyping and stereotyping maintains power. In this case, applying the principle of 'mutual vulnerability' within an educational context will reveal the material functioning of how power encourages and is maintained by stereotyping" (p. 110).

Brantmeier's (2013) pedagogy of vulnerability is framed around higher education, but I suggest that it can and should be used for K–12 education as well; in fact, I believe it is even more impactful when used at this foundational stage of schooling. In Brantmeier's approach, educators allow themselves to be vulnerable by putting themselves in a position of learning alongside their student; they embrace knowing what they do not know. This approach to education requires that educators share their stories, thereby creating a lived curriculum—what Brantmeier refers to as "the content of our lives, the past lived experiences, that have become the foundation of learning new concepts, skills, and values" (p. 3). A lived curriculum comes from both the educator and the learner, further amplifying reciprocal ways of knowing, being, and sharing the classroom.

"When education is the practice of freedom, students are not the only ones who are asked to share and to confess," writes hooks (1994). "Any classroom that employs a holistic model of learning will also be a place where teachers grow and are empowered by the process. That empowerment cannot happen if we refuse to be vulnerable while encouraging students to take risks" (p. 21). Might we all acknowledge that in this leadership journey, we may not always go down the right path at first, but we should try to avoid going down the wrong ones very far? We need to provide those we love with the grace and the space to risk and to fail—to be vulnerable—relying on our scaffolding to help them find the right path for themselves.

Miller and colleagues (2011) offer commentary on the work of Paulo Freire, insisting that educators need to view marginalized and oppressed students as the ones who are the most capable of framing their own experiences and demanding appropriate change. "[T]hose who have experienced the brunt of oppressive structures (such as immigrants, people of color, and/or people who are poor) have long been deemed incapable of creating change and working for the betterment of their own conditions and society in general" (p. 1083). Approaching education and leadership with humility and openness casts aside the notions of superiority and supremacy that so often dominate school settings and opens the way for love, caring, and vulnerability.

In progressive education, love, care, and vulnerability are essential components for creating a safe and supportive learning environment. Love creates a sense of belonging, helps foster positive relationships, and encourages students to be more open and expressive. Care generates an atmosphere where students feel valued and appreciated and where their well-being and mental health are prioritized. Vulnerability allows students and their teachers to be open, honest, and authentic about their thoughts, feelings, and experiences and creates a space where they feel comfortable taking risks and making mistakes. When these elements are present, students are more likely to develop a strong sense of self-worth and confidence in their learning process that will enable them to delve deeper and go further in their learning journey.

To Rosa Morales (Josue's Mom)

Dear Rosa,

I hope you, Johnny, and the family are doing well. It's been several years since we last saw each other at Josue's memorial basketball tournament, during The Met's anniversary celebration in Providence. I still can't believe my team lost the championship game! Especially given how much I stacked my team with former players—many of whom also played in college, and all of whom knew Josue. I remember the moment when a couple of the players walked over and said, "I never miss those shots, Coach." It became clear that your team, Josue's church team, was meant to win this tournament. I suppose it makes sense, given their connection to Josue, your church, and your family. I don't doubt that Josue was the angel shaking the backboard and blowing heavy winds every time our team took a shot. Or maybe he was on the court as the mysterious sixth player for the other team, poking the ball away from some of my most accomplished players. Knowing Josue, I'm sure he got a really good laugh out of the entire thing. I believe he would have also loved how both teams huddled after the game to pray and give thanks for him and the times we all had with him. In the end, it was an absolutely beautiful day and a most appropriate way to celebrate him.

I periodically check in on Rocio via Facebook. She and I chat from time to time. It's nice to see the young, spiritual woman she has come to be. I recall Josue speaking about her before she came to The Met. He used to say, "She's a beast, man. She's no joke." I have to say he was right about his baby sister. She was a handful—though she always had strong values and simply would not allow anyone to just tell her anything. Please give her a big hug for me and let her know I'm proud of her.

I've been meaning to reach out to you for quite some time. I frequently think of Josue and regularly share stories about him when I talk to others around the country about working with young people. I think back to the many moments he and I had together during his time at The Met. The most infamous moment, of course, is the Parmesan cheese debacle. I still can't quite understand how he completely emptied an industrial-sized bottle of Parmesan cheese inside the van! The image of the entire floor and seating areas covered with smelly white cheese is hilariously funny now. I remain impressed to this day by how quickly he assumed responsibility for his actions and accepted the research project on cheese I assigned him as a "learning opportunity." There is no doubt in my mind you had a lot to do with how he handled it. I always appreciated your support as a parent and the way we were partners when it came to supporting Josue.

I remember his very first exhibition, which took place shortly after the cheese incident. He looked sharp, as he always did when he wore a shirt and tie. Ironically, for someone who always showed up so cool, he was visibly nervous that day. His nerves got the best of him, and he became frustrated with the process and his level of preparedness. In the middle of the exhibition, when Josue was struggling a bit, a colleague slipped me a note that said, "He will be one of your shining stars." In that moment, I remember feeling uncertain and thinking, "We'll see." I did not yet know how right he was.

One of my fondest memories with Josue is the trip he and I took to Orlando in 2004 to speak at the ASCD Annual Conference. Dennis Littky was the headliner, of course, but it was Josue who stole the show. There were more than a thousand people in the room; it was the largest crowd I had ever spoken in front of at that point. Josue spoke passionately about you and how you supported him and his sisters, and showed beautiful vulnerability when talking about his dad, the impact of his dad's incarceration on him, and his commitment to creating a different path for himself.

The trip was the first time Josue and I were able to have a long, uninterrupted time together focused on matters other than school. The two of us had dinner together at a Florida-themed restaurant, pink flamingos and all. I had to reassure him that he could order whatever he wanted from the menu because The Met would reimburse me. That he had an awareness of and sensitivity to such matters truly touched my heart. We talked about so much that evening—basketball, obviously, but also about our session together, providing each other support and feedback. He was slightly bashful, yet beamed with pride as people came to our table to share their appreciation and respect for his presentation. That day, he confidently accepted business cards from strangers who had witnessed his brilliance. We both appreciated the moment. He felt proud, and rightfully so. I was likewise proud and know you were as well.

We had so many incredible experiences together that now serve as fond memories on my most challenging days. I truly miss him and think of him often. He taught me how to be a better father. I learned patience and compassion being his advisor. Josue's unyielding faith in God and his belief in something greater than himself inspired me. Because of Josue, I'm a better person. He helped shape my perspective and outlook on life. From him, I learned the value of not taking everything so seriously and the importance of laughter. Josue showed me that being silly, having fun, and being brilliant are not mutually exclusive. He was all those things!

Although you and I never discussed what led to Josue's passing, I still have the message you sent me that early September morning. I visit his Facebook page periodically; it feels like he's still with us. Friends and family post messages, pictures, and videos, affectionately calling him Josue, Josh, Swizz, or EQ—some of the many names he was known to answer to. Although it is not surprising how many people loved Josue, I remain in awe of the nearly one thousand people that attended his wake and funeral service. He was a natural leader who touched so many people's lives and brought them together.

Thank you for trusting me with educating your son. Thank you for showing me love by holding me accountable to do my best to educate Josue, while also demonstrating compassionate love in the thoughts and prayers you expressed when my daughter Bella was born. From you, I learned that every child is someone's perfectly imperfect child, and that I was expected to show up and be my best self. I'm sad that Bella wasn't old enough to remember meeting and laughing with Josue. They are kindred spirits in so many ways. She would have loved him, he would have adored her.

I want you to know that I will continue to celebrate Josue and his life. I will continue sharing his gifts with the world. I will continue to live with the greatest of appreciation while maintaining a healthy perspective on life and remembering to laugh. Josue would have it no other way.

Hablamos pronto, y que el señor lo cuides a usted y su familia (Let's speak soon, and may God continue to watch over you and your family).

With love,

Carlos

4 | Josue

Love is patient, love is kind. It does not envy, it does not boast, it is not proud. It does not dishonor others, it is not self-seeking, it is not easily angered, it keeps no record of wrongs. Love does not delight in evil but rejoices with the truth. It always protects, always trusts, always hopes, always perseveres. Love never fails.

—Corinthians 13:4–8

Remember: give love first.

—Michael Washor

It is rare to have a student who intimidates you before you actually meet. There are few students who *truly* challenge and test your patience, but often they are the ones who have the greatest impact on you. For me, that student was Josue.

A charismatic young man, Josue had a personality and presence that were larger than life. I saw so much of myself in Josue. As a 6-foot-3 9th grader, he towered over his classmates. Neither of us, however, used our physical size to intimidate. It was quite the opposite, in fact: Josue's lighthearted, playful, and sensitive nature uniquely defined him. He was confident in his playfulness while also guarded and self-protective out of a fear of rejection.

I first met Josue during The Met's Summer Infusion—a two-week summer bridge program for incoming 9th grade students. He immediately drew my attention—and that of anyone else within earshot—because he was being fiercely cursed out by another student during a community cleanup activity. I thought to myself, *There is no way anyone could make another person that upset.* I dismissed it as a squabble among teens and thought nothing more of it.

The following day, parents were invited for an evening event that marked the culmination of the Summer Infusion program. During the ceremony, I found myself sitting next to Josue in the back of the room. Without hesitation, he said, "You're big."

"Yes," I responded. "You're big, too."

I asked him if his parents were there, and he pointed to a tall, elegant woman who was listening intently to what the school would provide for her son and the other incoming students. Her attentiveness caused me to think to myself, *If this kid is in my advisory, I will have a dedicated parent and ally.* Then I remembered the scolding he'd received the day before and secretly hoped he would be placed with someone else. Josue did become my advisee—and while there were certainly a few trying moments, I'm eternally grateful.

Having Josue as a student in my advisory taught me a lot about myself as a leader. Through him, I learned how to lead with intention. I will forever remember our advisory's 9th grade camping trip, when my leadership was truly tested. It was then that I discovered the importance of guiding with compassion and responding from love rather than reacting from frustration. During the camping trip, one of our tents was ruined because a student used their finger to poke holes in it. I reluctantly agreed to allow four young men—including Josue—to sleep in the van instead. After we finished cooking and eating spaghetti with marinara sauce and Parmesan cheese, we ended the evening and packed the food and supplies in the van. Before going to sleep in my tent, I said very clearly that I did not want to be awakened by loud talking and noise and that they should not touch any items in the van.

Less than 30 minutes later, I was jolted up by loud gasps and gagging coming from the boys as they exited the van, fleeing a Parmesan cheese cloud and waving their hands in front of their noses, their mouths gasping desperately for fresh air. As I approached the scene, I encountered Josue laughing hysterically. It was apparent he was the culprit, having intentionally sprinkled the entire contents of an industrial-size container while goofing around with his advisory mates.

This incident epitomizes Josue: a physically large but innocent comedian with a mischievous spirit. I can laugh in retrospect, but at that moment, I was hot. It would have been easy for me to respond in a punitive way, doling out a suspension or expulsion. Instead, I chose to use the incident as an opportunity to reflect and learn. I assigned Josue a 10-page research paper on cheese. He was expected to investigate and write all about various types of cheese—where different cheeses originate, how they are made, and so on. At the conclusion of the assignment, Josue had deepened his research and writing skills while continuously reflecting on his behavior. His final paper was nicely done, and his mother, Rosa, supported him throughout the process of writing and researching it.

I also recall a time (shared in the letter) when Josue joined me and Dennis Littky for a presentation at an ASCD conference in Florida. Josue was Dennis's opening act; I added a bit of commentary. Josue started the session off strong, amazing the large audience with his presence, insights, and candor. He set the stage for Dennis so well. The evening before his presentation, Josue and I went to dinner and reviewed his speech notes. We also got into some deep conversations about his family and mine and how he was dealing with challenges as he was making his way in the world. I like to think that the love, care, and vulnerability we shared during that dinner helped prepare him for his successful presentation.

What Josue Needed

Josue was passionate and determined to be successful for himself and for his family. He grew and thrived while at The Met. Although he sometimes doubted his academic preparedness in comparison with his peers, his impressive vocabulary and near-photographic memory enabled him to compensate. He worked hard at The Met and was admitted into his dream school (and my alma mater), Johnson & Wales University.

Like many students who are the first in their family to attend college, Josue struggled to make the transition. His mother would recall to me later that she did not think he was ready for a four-year institution. Several studies have shown that first-generation students lack confidence in their academic abilities to successfully persist and perform in college (Engle & Tinto, 2008). The first year was especially difficult, as Josue was challenged by conventional lecture-style courses and more abstract academic content while also attempting to navigate a large, complex system. Grappling with the difficulties of negotiating college life, Josue became disenchanted and disengaged. He fell into a depressive state, and one day, for reasons unknown to anyone, he and an acquaintance robbed a convenience store.

Josue was sentenced to a year in prison. Although it wasn't a lengthy sentence, he emerged forever changed by the experience. He remained consumed by regret, saddled with a felony, and his dreams of a postsecondary education were thwarted.

Much like his mother, I can only speculate as to why Josue decided to commit robbery. It's possible that the challenges of college felt insurmountable. Although we will never know, I often reflect on how I could have better supported Josue in making the transition from The Met to college. What is obvious in retrospect is that Josue needed love, care, and compassion during a particularly vulnerable period in his life. It leaves me to wonder how to build better bridges between our secondary and postsecondary institutions to support our most vulnerable students.

What Josue Taught Me

My instinct is to begin my work with students by focusing on relationship building. I follow the guidance of Ted Sizer, who stated that he could not teach a child whom he did not know well (2009). Before I am able to teach any of my students, I must first develop a relationship with them. This was especially true with Josue. In my work with Josue, I knew that I had to build a relationship with him before we could come together to hone our respective leadership skills. I am not automatically entitled to guide, teach, or lead any of my students; I must earn the privilege.

Once I'd made a connection with Josue, I could begin to push the boundaries of my teaching and his learning. At the beginning of our relationship, I asked myself how I could contribute to Josue's life in ways that mattered to him. *Leading is about enabling others to achieve their highest and greatest purpose.* For me to support Josue, it was essential that I intentionally craft a mutually beneficial relationship. I was reflective and purposeful about how I supported his learning and development, identifying opportunities for us to interact so that we could get to know each other (our shared loves of basketball and hip-hop were two of those opportunities).

Josue had a tendency to drag and shuffle his feet, which made it seem like he had no destination or purpose. "*Recoje los pies,*" I told him. "*Los hombres no ratrean los pies* (Pick up your feet. Men don't drag their feet)." When I was a child, my father had told me the same thing. Because Josue knew that I cared about him, we were able to discuss the story behind my father saying those words to me and discuss the literal and figurative meaning of what it means to move with purpose.

Josue modeled for me and others the complexity of living by your values grounded by an unwavering faith. Josue's steadfast religious beliefs made him a natural leader. It is rare to find someone so young who possesses that level of public conviction. But early in our interactions, I recognized that his leadership skills extended beyond religion. Josue was astute at fitting in, always perceived as cool and popular. He had a natural ability to inspire his peers, although like many young boys, he did not always demonstrate it. I and others encouraged him to write and reflect on his behavior and future aspirations—to share his ideas, wonderings, and concerns of the heart. His writings revealed the tension between living in dual and sometimes competing worlds—his faith-centered time at church events and time spent at school and in the community with his many friends. They also revealed that he never compromised his faith in favor of popularity. Over the years, I observed Josue grow into his faith. He began speaking publicly, including to friends, about his beliefs. I admired his resolve as he successfully blurred the lines between the worlds he worked so carefully to navigate.

Takeaways on Leadership and Love

Unfortunately, Josue's story does not have a happy ending; he passed away due to an accidental overdose of prescription medication. It is, however, a story about love. Josue taught me that leadership is best when buoyed by love, and that students deserve relationships with loving and caring educators who prioritize their learning needs. Here are just a few of the things I learned from my relationship with Josue:

- **The importance of understanding cultural experiences and perspectives.** While Josue and I shared a lot of similar experiences and physical attributes, Josue provided unique insights into challenges that I never faced (including domestic violence in the home and an incarcerated parent).
- **The benefits of resilience and determination.** Male students of color often face significant obstacles, but Josue's resilience and determination to succeed served as an inspiration to me.
- **The impact of implicit biases.** Students of color often experience the negative effects of implicit biases from teachers and other authority figures. Implicit biases can influence a teacher's expectations, assessment, and treatment of students. Josue reported to me that in his previous educational experiences, teachers had lower expectations for him and disciplined him more harshly than his peers. Josue experienced such biases throughout his K–8 schooling. Because of this, he often assumed

that he would be the first suspect in any case of mischief. Understanding how young people see and respond to these biases can help teachers take steps to combat them.

- **The importance of representation.** Josue told me that one of the reasons he felt particularly connected to me was that I was the rare teacher who looked like him and shared similar experiences. In his case, that bond led to increased motivation, improved engagement in school, and more satisfaction with learning.

- **New perspectives and teaching techniques.** Josue, like many male students of color, had unique learning styles and approaches to education. Because I was able to invest the time in getting to know him and his family circumstances well, we could collaborate on ideas and techniques to better engage and support him in his learning.

To Angelis León (Angel's Daughter)

Dear Angelis,

Although you and I haven't met, I have known about you since you were born. Your mom and dad were students of mine. I knew them before they were fortunate enough to conceive you. In fact, I was your dad's high school principal for two years. Over the years, I've heard such amazing things about you from your mom. I recently reached out to her to see if it was OK to write to you. I hope it's OK with you, too.

I continue to work in education, although I am no longer a principal. My job is to help teachers and principals do great work with students like your mom and dad all around the world. I've been thinking a lot about your dad over the last few years and have shared some amazing stories about him with friends and colleagues, and even on stage in front of hundreds of people. Then I thought that I should share these stories with you! I want you to know the incredible impact your dad had on my life. He taught me and others that we should always look for and recognize the brilliance in our students, no matter where they come from. I also want to share how his life serves as a reminder and inspiration to educators and adults who work with young people around the country.

I'm sure you have heard stories about your dad from family members. About how smart, funny, and talented he was. Or how he loved playing basketball and rapping. I am sure countless people have shared that he always had a smile on his face. All those things are true, and I would like to share a few more personal stories about your dad.

Your dad was a protector who loved his family deeply. I often sat in meetings with your dad and your grandmother, Carmen. My father and your grandmother were both born in the Dominican Republic, so we had a special Caribbean connection. Watching your dad show acts of kindness and care to your grandmother was truly a special thing. He made sure she wasn't worried about the small things that parents always worry about, like finishing homework and getting sleep. And he helped her around the house by running errands so she wouldn't have to strain.

He was also very protective of his younger brothers (your uncles). He tried to be a provider and a protector for both of them, even though they were only a few years younger.

Your dad was a talented and persuasive writer. When he wrote about things he cared about, your dad could make an incredibly convincing case, even to adults. He had a passion for research and writing. For example, here is the opening paragraph to an essay he wrote in the 9th grade; he loved hip-hop and wanted to share with other people how he saw it changing:

> During the late 1970s until the 1990s, hip-hop was more of a trend that combined art, fashion, and music but most of all knowledge and individuality. In the 21st century, the meaning of hip-hop has changed from a culture of knowledge and individuality to a culture of materialism and commonality.

Your dad's former advisor, Patty, shared several of his written pieces and essays. If you would like to see them, I would enjoy sending them to you. I believe you would enjoy reading them and gaining insight into how he thought about things.

Your dad was a natural leader. He was the type of leader who made others around him want to be better. He and I often talked about his ambition and the goals he had for himself and his family. He loved being with and around people, and people enjoyed his company. His classmates at The Met loved him and deeply respected him. His friends regularly looked to him for his opinion and support when they were having problems.

Your dad would have been an awesome father. I remember that the last time I bumped into him in Providence, he was super excited to share that he was going to be a dad. He wanted to do well. He really wanted to have a family, and he wanted to make a positive impact on the world. The look in his eyes that day was unlike anything I had seen before from him. Remembering his kindness and care with his mom, brothers, and close friends gives me tremendous comfort and confidence that he would have done anything and everything in his power to ensure that you were loved, happy, and safe. I sincerely hope that you hear this often from the many family members and friends who knew and loved your dad. He was truly great. I believe your mom saw these qualities in him as well. In fact, she shares some of those qualities, which means that these qualities live in you, too, Angelis.

Your father taught me to be a better educator. I tell stories about your dad to other teachers and principals to show that adults must listen deeply to young people. Some of the lessons I learned from him were tough ones with even tougher consequences. My hope is that sharing his story—our story—with other adults will help them be more patient when working with students like your dad. Hopefully they will not rush to judgment when the students they love make mistakes.

I've enclosed a small gift that I hope you will enjoy. One of my daughter Isabella's favorite books is Brown Girl Dreaming by Jacqueline Woodson. It's a beautiful true story about a Brown girl—like you—who experiences sadness and pain but finds a way to grow and blossom.

My hope is that this book shows you that all parts of our story make us amazingly beautiful and complex people. I hope that you continue to find your voice and, over the years, learn how to use it in ways that make sense to you and to those you care most about. May you find joy in the memories of those, like your dad, who made it possible for you to live out their most awesome and wildest dreams.

Please hug your mom for me. I look forward to meeting you in person one day.

With love,

Carlos

5 | Angel

> When we are unwilling to confront these harsh realities of social
> inequality with our pedagogy—to cultivate their "control of destiny"—
> all we have left to offer youth is hope deferred. This offer comes when
> we ask our students to set their sights on some temporally distant (and
> highly unlikely) future well-being.
>
> —Jeffrey R. Duncan-Andrade

When I think about Angel León and my time with him at The Met,
I remember a young man mature beyond his years—someone who
was carrying heavy burdens that no young person should have to
shoulder. His personal circumstances were exacerbated by societal
woes, including exposure to violence and limited opportunities.
Unfortunately, Angel was not an anomaly. Our society does a great
disservice to Black and Brown children and young adults.

Angel never had the opportunity meet Angelis, his daughter, as he
was tragically shot and killed while sitting in a barbershop before she
was born. In writing my letter to her, I wanted Angelis to know that her
father was so much more than his unfortunate ending. He was dynamic
in so many ways and, while he is no longer with us, I believe that he lives
on through her. She may not have had the opportunity to know him, but
my hope is that she will know a little bit more about who he was.

Who Angel Was

Born in New York City, Angel León was the son of Dominican immigrants Carmen and Ricardo León and the second youngest of four

brothers. From a very early age, Angel possessed a passion and love for visual arts, music, poetry, and sports. As a little boy, he was happy and incredibly curious. During most of his youth, his parents, who were much older, moved Angel and his brothers back and forth between New York City and Providence in search of a better life for their family. Providence offered a tightly knit Latinx community filled with entrepreneurs of color and transplanted New Yorkers who felt that the cozy confines of the city provided them with the best opportunities for their children.

In 2006, at the age of 14, Angel was a 9th grader at The Met. As soon as he came aboard, Angel knew he wanted to pursue his passion for art. He immediately began developing a portfolio of his sketches, most of which connected to his interests in architecture and nontraditional structures. His dream internship was to work with artists at the world-renowned Rhode Island School of Design. Angel was brilliant, as are *all* our young brothers of color who grow up in inner cities and are too often overlooked. He could spit the grimiest rhymes off the dome and then pen an eloquent and thoughtful reflection on the history and current state of hip-hop. He was just that versatile. From day one, Angel showed a self-awareness unique in someone so young that enabled him to put up a shield of self-preservation in the face of difficulties.

At The Met, Angel was placed in an advisory with my colleague Patty Bamford. They were an unlikely pair—Patty, a white woman of deep Irish heritage, and Angel, an Afro-Latino young man—but they built a positive rapport right out of the gate. Angel deferred to Patty in ways he did not defer to anyone else, students or adults. They cared deeply for one another and had each other's backs. Here's how Patty described her first encounter with Angel:

> Angel was assigned to my group in Summer Infusion, and I remember he stood out from the start. [He was] very vocal and wanted to make people laugh—and he succeeded. He could be a clown, but was also witty . . . he had a great sense of humor. (Personal communication, 2021)

Angel secured an internship quickly. An avid reader and lover of literature, he leveraged his relationship with his middle school librarian—a woman of color—to set up an opportunity as a librarian's assistant. He excelled in that role, using his combined love of the arts and reading to assist with creating book displays and events for middle schoolers, working and learning directly from his mentor.

But something changed for Angel. He abruptly left his internship at the library and moved on to a new one. Patty recalled:

> He began interning with a local barber and he was really excited about it. He was like, "Enough library, this is my passion." I didn't want to stand in his way, but I didn't get the same positive vibe as the library. It wasn't a bad vibe at the barber's, but it was different. It wasn't as structured, and I wanted to make sure he was actually learning and not just hanging out.

What happened to Angel's dreams of becoming an architect? Suddenly he seemed more concerned with a career that would earn him quick money. Angel was resourceful by both nature and necessity. In addition to being poetic with his words, he had some serious hustle.

How Angel Lived

Angel's home life was tumultuous, as is often the case for families living in poverty. With two elderly parents, Angel was often left to his own devices, which meant having to provide for himself. The responsibility of providing for his parents often fell on him as well. In a study on Latino masculinity, Hurtado and colleagues (2012) found that "Latino families often pushed sons into premature independence, many times with little guidance or family supervision. An early independence from curfews and strictly enforced rules is often conceptualized as male privilege, but many respondents in the study expressed confusion and loneliness from the unguided freedom their families granted them" (p. 111). Angel's family structure dictated that early independence was his destiny—a scary place for someone who was still very much a child.

When he entered The Met as a freshman, Angel was introduced to a holistic network of educators who cared for students as though they were family. The Met nurtured Angel and provided the stability that he was missing. Through his advisory he found a routine, yet he was still very private about things that we as adults should have been able to help him with. Unlike traditional schools, we included our students' families and community in our curriculum and outreach. Unfortunately, Angel was dealing with things that Patty and I were never aware of. His former girlfriend, Sabrina—who would later become the mother of his daughter—revealed to me in later years that Angel was often struggling with basic survival. He never missed a day of school, because that's where he got his meals. Sabrina also explained that he often carried all his possessions with him, worried that his two older brothers would steal them, send them to the Dominican Republic, or sell them. Angel's reality made the choices he made in school that much more significant.

Angel's behavior in school underwent a major shift once he began his internship at the barbershop. What was once a supportive and positive relationship between Patty and Angel had now become strained. According to Patty, Angel wanted to do things his way or no way at all. He dug his heels in and dared anyone to move him. Patty described his attitude toward schooling and participation:

> I think that the participation . . . became less productive, less positive. He was more argumentative with me and with other students in the advisory. It felt like he was reaching a level of frustration, and maybe it was coming out against other people. Also, I just saw him begin to take on this, you know, "fuck it" sort of attitude. Like kind of throwing his hands up and saying, "Yeah, I'll go through the motions, but this is bullshit."

What we should have known at the time was that this behavior was a plea for help. Somehow, we were unable to recognize it as such and respond in a way that would engage Angel more effectively. While I can only speculate, my sense is that Angel was frustrated and unsure of his options, both immediate and long term. He was acting out because he was a child having to contend with serious adult issues. Linda Burton (2007) speaks to the adultification of children in low-income families and the premature and often inappropriate exposure to adult issues and responsibilities within their families. As time went on, Angel became one of those students who pushed buttons and challenged how true the school was to its motto of "One student at a time."

My care for Angel led me to accommodate his boundary pushing. I gave him access to my office for quiet time and focused work. I often had him serve as a guide for visitors to the school, a task he relished. And he reciprocated—for example, by showing genuine care for me when I was dealing with some of my daughter's medical issues. I thought that my demonstrations of care for him would compensate for its absence in most of his other relationships and result in mutual trust. I expected that demonstrating genuine care would help to build a strong relationship that Patty and I could leverage to motivate Angel to engage in learning.

I did what I thought was right at the time to support Angel. As a young and inexperienced administrator, I vehemently advocated for Angel with staff who questioned whether The Met was the right school for him. I defended him and believed in him. After all, that is what called me to this organization—the opportunity to show up for young people, including those that were like me. All of this was true.

Until the day Angel stole and sold my laptop.

He broke my trust—but even then, I was still willing to give him a chance. I told him to simply admit that he had taken the laptop and return it. I would have been less concerned with the laptop had it not been for the irreplaceable images stored on it. My child, Isabella, was born premature at 24 weeks—a mere 1 pound, 14 ounces. On that laptop were my earliest images of her first four months of life. I pleaded with Angel through a combination of rage and tears, but he refused to cop to stealing the computer. In my desperation to recover it, I investigated and gathered evidence that confirmed that he had taken it. I even went so far as to visit his home and speak with his mother, who confirmed that her son had brought home a laptop that did not belong to him. My laptop and the memories that I hoped to one day share with Bella were gone.

I became unhinged. I made the unilateral decision to "put him out." He had to go. Angel no longer could be part of the community at The Met. I scheduled an exit meeting with Angel and his family to discuss alternate education options for him, but they never showed—and I never followed up.

What Angel Needed

In retrospect, I can see that what Angel needed was a more intense style of mentorship. While mentoring is built into the Big Picture Learning model, I think we missed the mark with Angel. He needed a mentor he could relate to—a male of color with shared life experiences. The signs were there, but somehow, we missed them—or, worse, I didn't pay attention to them. He should have had someone who could advocate on his behalf and meet his needs.

Noguera (2012) extols the importance of mentoring for Black and Latino males:

> Our research in [low-income] schools showed us that strong, positive relationships between teachers and students are critical ingredients of their success. Equally important is the need to provide a personalized learning environment with mentors, counseling, and supports that make it possible for schools to intervene early and effectively when problems arise. (p. 11)

It is my belief that Patty lacked the tools she needed to support Angel, and as her principal, it was my responsibility to see that. My role was to support her as a new advisor and leader. Together, we might have been able to identify what she needed and build those tools, which might have resulted in a better outcome. She was not the first white woman (nor will she be the last) to have difficulty supporting young men of color. I should have known better, as I was only one year removed from the role of advisor myself. Advisors and teachers cannot be, nor should they be, all things to all students. But I should have asked Angel about whether any strong Black or Latino men formed a part of his learning community outside school. He lacked mentorship, and he should have been able to come to me. Ideally, I could have provided him with access to other mentors or community partners to support him.

What Angel needed was leadership embedded in care. That is not to say that I did not care for Angel—quite the contrary. But I did not understand how to care for him in a way that could have changed the direction of his life. Care for Angel should have included more intensive interventions and other supports. Low-income students have unique care requirements. While The Met addressed a lot of those basic needs, such as making sure students received two meals a day, had opportunities for counseling and adult mentorship, and could find spaces for mediation when necessary, Angel needed much more. Big Picture Learning schools are predicated on serving the whole child, which includes their families and communities, and while imperfect, I am proud of how we continue to grow, learn, and improve on how to better and more holistically support our young people. As Angel's principal, I should have done more to show him the care that he deserved and needed. I was simply unaware of all that Angel faced.

What Angel Taught Me

I cannot, in good conscience, absolve Angel of all his actions during his time at The Met. After all, he did steal and sell something of deep meaning to me. But I can reflect on and question whether we—myself included—gave him the care he truly needed. I took his theft of my computer very personally as a violation of trust. Yet, in hindsight, I question whether things would have reached such a boiling point had I been more in tune with his needs. Angel's tough exterior made him seem impervious to intervention. But I could have gone to his house *before* he took my property; I could have done it when things took a turn in his behavior with Patty. I could have done regular check-ins with him when I learned that he was facing difficulty in his internships. I could have connected him with some of my local undergraduate fraternity brothers from similar backgrounds and experiences who were closer to Angel's age. He may have been unable to proactively communicate his circumstances to the adults in his life, but it was my job as leader and caregiver to pay closer attention to the signs and try to learn more about the underlying root causes of his behavior.

I believed my approach with Angel, as with other young boys of color at The Met, was built on mutual respect. I based our relationship on truth, honesty, and never correcting them in public unless it was absolutely called for. I tried to always communicate to him that he was loved. However, knowing what I know now, I wonder if I was fully there for him in the ways that he needed me to be. I wonder about the mentors that Angel had at his internships and whether he should have been more intentionally paired with a person and not just an industry. As a team, we should have thought about scouring southern New England for a male architect of color with lived experiences similar to Angel's. We all knew that Angel was in the streets, and I should have done more.

I learned from Angel that caring and responding to the express needs of students transcends whatever we are typically expected to do in the classroom; that caring should not be bound to school hours; that we must be willing to protect students' bodies and hearts from harm and trauma. Even when this is not possible, I learned that we must be there to help them heal from these inevitable life experiences.

Angel's story illustrates that caring is more than empathy and concern. It's about specific actions that are motivated by love and tuned to the needs and circumstances of the individual young person. I struggled to help Angel because I misread his needs for care, and I was unprepared to supply the level of care he needed. Did Angel need more fatherly care to balance what a mentor might provide? Did I miss faint signals that the school and I were falling short? How should leaders understand and respond to the subtleties of the needs of students like Angel? Developing such an understanding is at the core of Leadership Soul.

To Shawn Gooding

My dude,

Let's get right to it! That's how you and I always did it! I miss you, and it hurts every time I realize you're not here. There have been so many times over the last two years I've wanted to text or call you to let you know that I was coming to Providence. Whenever I would call, you would spring into action and notify other members of our advisory ("The Usual Suspects," we used to call ourselves—and still do—but we were always so much more than that!) so that we could all get together. You were the glue that bonded our entire advisory together, including significant others and children. You would regularly remind the advisory that we were overdue for a reunion and that we needed to visit Paddy's Beach Club for food and drinks and to hang out. It should come as no surprise to learn that the last time most of The Usual Suspects got together was on April 27, in Westerly, to celebrate your homegoing. "So _this_ is what it takes to get all of you to come down to South County," you'd say if you were there. I'm sorry I didn't come down sooner.

Now that you're gone, I realize how much I've missed having you check on me through Facebook, texts, or phone calls. You were always intentional about staying in touch. Whenever I came to town, you would drive me around in your truck. I recall one time, shortly after you turned 21, you reminded me of your age while offering me Jack Daniels. I still remember the look I gave you to signify that, whatever your age, you and I were not going to drink together in your truck. Even though I was your advisor—or perhaps _because_ I was—we didn't have _that_ type of relationship.

I'm sorry we never had that drink together.

Your parents planned an amazing program to celebrate your life. They did a great job creating a space for everyone to say goodbye to you. I truly cannot imagine the pain that they were in that day. It took two whole days for everyone to cry and laugh as we gathered to trade stories about our time with you. Your beautiful homegoing brought hundreds of people together, wearing multiple shades of purple to create a display of royalty in your honor while lifting up your life and your gifts. Everyone honored your beautiful spirit and talked about your authenticity. Several people stood up during the service and shared fond stories of you, while others waited until food and drinks were in hand to laugh and share. A few folks even popped bottles in your honor in the parking lot while exchanging embarrassing stories. It was a perfect way to celebrate you and your life.

I was honored that your parents invited me to speak at your service. They wanted me to share about the person, student, and man that I had come to know, love, and respect. Our relationship began with you as a student at The Met and it continued into your early adult years. We both know that the journey wasn't always easy. I sincerely hope you felt proud of what you accomplished and how much you grew over the years. I was inspired by the man you were becoming.

I'm sorry I didn't tell you enough how proud I was of you.

I learned something new about you at the service, despite having known you for 16 years. Maybe "new" isn't the right word. Perhaps it's more accurate to say that I realized that everyone who met you and had the honor of having spent time with you felt a unique and special relationship with you. A few thought of you as their best friend, while many more thought of you as a good friend. That's the way you made people feel, Shawn. It was real; it wasn't a con. You never had an agenda other than to be your authentic self. The shit was genuine. It was heartfelt, and people sensed that. I mean, your obituary conveyed exactly what so many of us witnessed:

> His family and friends will deeply miss his outgoing and vibrant personality. He was as charming as he was good-looking. Friends were like family to him. Wherever Shawn went in Westerly, people knew him and called him by name. Shawn believed his purpose in life was to make people happy and to be there for them. Whether they needed a ride to work, emotional support, or someone to take charge during a crisis, Shawn was the go-to guy.

I was honored that I got to meet so many people who were important to you in your life.

Your mom and I stay in touch a bit more than we used to. She is one of the strongest women I've ever met, and I know she misses you deeply. Your father and I got to speak briefly during the wake. Your brother and sister were there, and they each shared beautiful words in your honor. I even had the chance to meet your biological father, who introduced himself to me after the services concluded. You and I never talked much about him, but I pray that you and he made whatever amends were needed so that you could each be at peace.

Your absence left a void for many, including your friends and advisory mates Brandon and Chris. Your boys. They both struggled to deal with your loss, which is understandable given how close y'all were. Initially I was worried about both of them, although I was especially concerned about Brandon. He took your death really hard. He and I stay in touch more often than we used to, which is a good thing. In fact, the whole advisory checks in on him regularly, which is also a good thing. Brandon always reminds me that you and Dan were his best friends, that you all had grown so close, and that he lost you both in very similar ways. Although he is a strong person, the advisory—his village—continues to support him.

I'm sorry I didn't reach out more to you after Dan's passing.

Jake was there, too, Shawn. I actually found the text you sent me when he was born:

Los—I have a son! Jake Matthew Hason Gooding born June 3rd at 6:22 PM 8 lbs. 12 ounces 19 inches long.

He looks so much like you, Shawn. He has your striking good looks and your boyish charm. I remember the last time I saw you both together, during The Met's 20th anniversary celebration. You brought Jake out to breakfast with the rest of the advisory and it totally tripped me out to watch you be a doting and affectionate dad. It's not surprising that your headstone has a beautiful picture of you and Jake carved into it. During the services, he seemed to be trying to make sense of it all: what was this new life and world going to be without his dad? Without his hero? I hold comfort knowing that your parents are incredibly involved, as are your brother and a number of your friends. I also know you'll continue to watch over him closely and be the angel he deserves.

The town of Westerly, the place you called home, has launched a number of programs in response to your passing. They've started intentional mental health and suicide prevention training across the city. Westerly Hospital's Washington County Suicide Prevention Program has organized several outreach sessions with your friends and family at Paddy's, The Malted Barley, and Cleats Sports Club—some of your favorite hangout spots. Just as anyone can be trained in CPR, anyone can be trained in suicide prevention. In addition, Westerly Public Schools has committed to getting their entire staff (more than 500 people) trained in Youth Mental Health First Aid in the coming year, and all police officers are now mandated to take the course.

I can't begin to imagine the pain you were in, Shawn. I'm sorry I wasn't aware of all that you were battling. I'm sorry I wasn't aware of your struggles and what you needed. Your beloved community of friends have committed themselves to making sure your memory lives on. Your friends post to your Facebook page (which is still active) on a regular basis with stories, images, and messages of love for you, Jake, and your family. They've taken on your beloved catchphrase—"Love you, mean it"—and are holding "Love you, mean it" events throughout Rhode Island in your memory.

I will continue to do my best to be authentic in all that I do. I will attempt to be a blessing to others and accept the blessings that others offer me, as you did. To treat others with love, care, and grace, as you did. To live life to its fullest, as you did. To bring people together, as you did. To speak the truth, as you did.

I hope you're resting peacefully, in your power, and pain-free, King. Love you, mean it.

Always,

Los

6 | Shawn

Shawn Gooding was an enigmatic young man with a heart of gold. He was constantly searching for his place in the world, his own little corner of belonging, and for him—as for many young people who struggle with depression and mental health issues—the search continued until the time of his passing. Like Josue and Angel, Shawn was a student of mine, but our relationship continued well past his time with me at the school. I knew Shawn through many stages of his brief but remarkable life. The letter I wrote to him, like the others in this book, helped me unpack my beliefs in this exploration of my Leadership Soul.

Who Shawn Was

At 13 years old, Shawn was the youngest student in my advisory and by far the smallest in stature. He had a sweet and playful innocence about him. Over the next four years, I would find it a constant challenge to gain traction with Shawn, who was easily swayed by his peers.

Julie and Antonio Gooding, a biracial couple, had adopted Shawn and his older brother when the boys were very young. As parents, they were very dedicated to supporting him. Julie, in particular, was a fierce and constant advocate. Still, Shawn struggled with his identity as an adopted child. As part of my advisory, I learned very quickly that Shawn needed to be supported in his individuality, which meant that he required a lot of one-on-one time. Fortunately, I was able to provide the attention he needed because he showed me how he needed to be taught. It was not an easy task, though. I had to earn Shawn's trust, and that meant being vulnerable as a leader.

Julie also made sure that I knew what Shawn needed. Through many conversations with them both, I learned that Shawn craved leadership that was caring and empathetic. He also needed to be built up in an honest way that was never performative. Shawn thrived with real, honest, authentic, and reaffirming feedback. I could never playfully poke at Shawn like I could with some of the other boys in the advisory, nor could I ever reprimand him publicly.

As Shawn's teacher and advisor, I learned patience and grace. Shawn was dealing with a lot in his life, much of which I did not learn about until well after his passing. I knew a lot, but nowhere near the full breadth and depth of what he was truly experiencing. In the beginning, I struggled as his advisor because he turned my system on its head. And while the shakeup was not intentional on his part, it forced me to acknowledge that a student's needs could not always be fully met in a group setting. I had to be able to support Shawn individually.

Shawn was the youngest advisee in the group, but the best reader and writer. He would read more than 100 books during his time at The Met and always landed amazing internships. But beyond those accomplishments, getting him to do any type of "work" was difficult. His mother, The Met administration, and I always found ourselves asking what other accommodations could be made to support his preferred learning styles. I knew that I wanted each of my students at the end of our time together to have strong time-management skills and be thoughtful about competing priorities, approaching tasks in a way that provided a sense of accomplishment. Many of my students were able to work autonomously, and I often found myself confused as to why Shawn could not. Without malice, Shawn challenged every system and structure that I put in place for him to be successful, which was incredibly frustrating.

I had to choose to stop chasing Shawn around the school. I had 16 other students who were, for the most part, on task and taking their work seriously. In my mind, Shawn would just have to explain at his exhibition why he did not do well and didn't have much work to show. But somehow, about two or three weeks before a deadline, Shawn would shift into another gear. He would start turning in assignments—documentation from his internship, brilliant reflections on his learning, logs of the numerous books he had been reading—resulting in a solid exhibition filled with art, playfulness, and detail.

I learned in my first two years with him that Shawn's brilliance was delicate and in need of protection from a world that expected specificity and mechanics—and I included myself in that world. In Shawn's final two years, I moved from being the person who demanded things from Shawn to the one who tried to lift him up. What he was doing and learning, although different from the type of work most other students in our advisory engaged in, was still deep, rigorous, real, and impressive. Were any other 15- and 16-year-olds working on rebuilding and restoring historic ships, developing amazing carpentry skills while also reading three to five books in a week? Creating human-sized puppets and masks and performing in festivals across the state? Taking college-level art classes and being recognized and acknowledged by their professors for their talents and diligent work?

Senior year was the hardest for both of us. It was my goal to ensure that my students graduated with clear postsecondary plans. Yet somewhere along the line, the connection between Shawn and me grew more tenuous. Chalk it up to me being a new father to a baby that was in the NICU for four months and to Shawn having a really difficult time at home, opting to sleep on various friends' couches across Rhode Island. He still came to school every day, but he was disengaged. I would later learn from Julie that Shawn had been dealing with several mental health crises. Yet in true Shawn style, he pulled through. At the end of the year, he delivered an exceptional capstone exhibition reflecting on his four years at The Met. He created an impressive gallery of ceramic replicas of historic Egyptian sculptures supported by a significant body of research. (These replicas were later featured at a gallery in Providence at the Rhode Island School of Design.)

When I think about Shawn and how he moved in this world, I reflect on how he consistently modeled positive behaviors in deep ways both in and out of school. Shawn exuded care for his peers and, in many instances, for me, especially once he had graduated. When I learned I was going to be a father, Shawn organized a group of students from my advisory to come over to my house and paint Isabella's room. When Isabella was born at 24 weeks, Shawn was the first student to call to make sure that I was doing all right. During the nearly four months that Isabella was in the NICU, Shawn regularly made her little drawings and crafts to put around her incubator.

Shawn took things to another level. He was always the one who would call me when there was something going on with any other member of our advisory. He reminded me of folks' birthdays. He let me know when one of my other students was having a hard time and needed to hear from me. He was also the one who helped organize celebrations when beloved friends passed away.

What Shawn Needed

In retrospect, I could have been more vulnerable with Shawn. I expected him to divulge a lot about himself, but I did not share my own colearning experiences with him. I could have shared how my own mentor, Mr. Montalban, stepped outside the classroom curriculum and taught me how to play chess and defend myself. In many ways, Shawn and I were opposites—I was always the biggest in stature among my classmates, and he was always the youngest and smallest among his. Yet despite these differences, we were more alike than I realized.

Though openly accessible in many ways, Shawn did not always trust easily. To gain his confidence required a mutual understanding that went beyond the classroom. I should have increased my openness with Shawn and opened the door for him to reciprocate. I think he needed me to go first when it came to communicating and showing vulnerability. His demonstrations of love through caring were outsized and frequent, but he needed me to share with him much more of my story, my journey, and my struggles.

Each of my students needed something different from me as their advisor. For some it was coaching or even just space to be. Others periodically required a bit more of a "full-court press" of support, scaffolding, and accountability. Although I couldn't always figure out what the right mix was for Shawn, through it all, I developed a deep love for him not just as a student but as a human. I truly gave a damn about him beyond what he was able to "produce." He needed me, the one charged with supporting him in his high school journey, to create safety for him. At times I met the mark. At other times I didn't quite get there.

What Shawn Taught Me

Shawn was incredibly vulnerable. He was a kind and reclusive young man who needed to be matched with an educator who was equally vulnerable. I had a lot of unlearning to do when it came to Shawn, particularly in that area, I had to learn how to be a vulnerable advisor. As Brantmeier (2013) notes in relation to the pedagogy of vulnerability, educators must allow themselves to be vulnerable in ways that allow teachers and students to colearn. I gained Shawn's trust by building our relationship in a way that accepted and honored his approach to learning.

Takeaways on Leadership and Vulnerability

I remember a veteran teacher warning me in my early years of teaching: "Don't get close to students. Don't open yourself to them, and don't encourage them to open themselves to you. Just teach them the course content and leave everything else at the classroom door." That teacher, unsurprisingly, is no longer in the profession.

That advice reminds me of Maslow's (1963) observation that a fear of knowing is also a fear of doing. To really know your students means you will lose sleep worrying about them and fretting about how you might help them. You will want to share who you are with them. You will want to reach out. Too many seasoned educators say, "Don't go there."

My own experience flips that advice on its head. Again, guided by Sizer (2009), I know that you cannot teach students—they will not *let you* teach them—unless you know them and know them well, *and they know you.* My belief in that axiom is strong, but my practice of it was sometimes weak. Still, my Leadership Soul demands that I express vulnerability, and it serves as a powerful position from which to express love and caring.

Educators have a responsibility to let their guard down with kids and really model what "not knowing" looks like. Do you share examples of times when things were hard for you or times you felt like you failed? Do you talk to kids about things you are not good at or are embarrassed to try? We educators need to be aware that in the course of every school day, we are repeatedly asking kids to do things that may make them uncomfortable or that they may not have done before. As adults, we often stop doing the things we are not good at and instead focus on improving at the things we are proficient at or enjoy. That freedom is not typically afforded to students, and they benefit from seeing the adults in their lives work through challenges.

Such openness must extend to the learning opportunities we codesign with our students so we can learn about, and build on, their interests and talents and help them take risks in their learning. Such openness, and careful scaffolding of that openness, leads students to learn and work at the edge of their confidence, competence, and commitment to extend all three. Teachers who embrace this vulnerability for themselves will find it easier to help their students embrace it as well.

Helping young people develop and exercise their agency requires that they feel some significant ownership of their learning and develop relationships with their teachers and others to codesign and pursue learning opportunities that empower even as they develop knowledge, skills, and dispositions. This quest for agency operates at every level, from the individual student to the entire community. We are all trying to matter and to make a difference. Love, care, and vulnerability are the tools we can use—*must* use—to help young people make their way in the world.

7 | A Commitment to Understanding and Action

> You don't make progress by standing on the sidelines, whimpering and complaining. You make progress by implementing ideas.
>
> —Shirley Chisholm

Reflection and applied learning are essential practices for developing Leadership Soul. Both require us to express love, care, and vulnerability with ourselves and others. The following principles can be adopted and adapted by individuals, programs, and institutions to support their development of Leadership Soul.

Allow Space for Reflection

I have too often found that leaders doing what I call "the work" don't give themselves the space for deep reflection. Leaders rarely have the opportunity to think over prior experiences, consult peers for feedback and input, or contemplate alternative or complex approaches to challenges.

Our schools consist of students, families, and educators with multiple interdependent identities, encompassing race, sexual orientation, language, religion, and socioeconomic status, among other characteristics. Leadership Soul requires leaders to be attuned to and respectful of these identities. Big Picture Learning supports leaders in moving beyond simply connecting work to theory or text. Our work helps ensure that leaders can reflect on their journeys—revisiting, recalling, and restating their original commitment to educating and uplifting young people.

In the Big Picture Learning network, we support such thoughtful analysis through a variety of initiatives and programs, including our school leadership coaching and additional adult learning initiatives, the Deep Learning Equity Fellowship and the Ashé Leaders Fellowship. One Big Picture Learning school principal, Brenda Diaz of Nashville Big Picture High School, reflected on how love, care, and vulnerability inform who she is as a leader and a person:

> Love, care, and vulnerability are the foundation of everything that I do as a leader of a high school with students from diverse populations. It is impossible for me to see the work without being empathetic. That empathy is about my own personal journey, but also the ability to sit in the seats of our students and families.

To support leaders in developing Leadership Soul, we focus on helping them understand the core of who they are as individuals and leaders and what motivates and inspires them to lead through thoughtful reflection. To lead with care and vulnerability requires deep listening, empathy, and compassion. In *Humble Leadership* (2018), authors Edgar Schein and Peter Schein ask, "Would it help to think of leadership not as the 'seven steps' you must take to lead, but as the energy that is shared in a group that is accomplishing something new and better?" Focusing on such opportunities requires a shift from "what I want to what is being asked of me" (p. 85).

Change the Context for Learning

We learn best when we engage in authentic learning experiences that include opportunities to reflect on our experiences and incorporate new knowledge, skills, and dispositions into our practice. To manifest this way of learning, aspiring leaders must do the following:

- **Create space for others to authentically lead.** When school leaders promote authentic leadership, they foster a sense of ownership and commitment among educators, staff, and students. Encouraging individuals to take the lead in areas where they are passionate and knowledgeable not only boosts their confidence but also leads to innovative approaches to problem solving and decision making. Giving students opportunities to authentically lead empowers them to take charge of their learning and personal growth. Encouraging student leadership also fosters self-confidence, responsibility, and a sense of accountability while creating a more inclusive learning environment in which young minds actively contribute to shaping their educational experience.

- **Implement a learner-centered focus and view students through an asset-based lens.** Viewing students as empty vessels in need of having knowledge poured into them creates an unproductive power dynamic. The educator becomes the primary "actor" in the classroom, and the student is the more passive recipient. Working with students to help them elucidate their interests and build on their strengths ensures that they are the primary actors building their muscles by doing the heavy lifting. The role of the educator and leader is more like the coach or spotter who monitors and encourages the learner.

- **Believe learning can occur anytime and anyplace, including outside school.** Far too often, educators overemphasize the importance of learning in the classroom and overlook the value of real-world experience. We must be sure to create education systems that acknowledge that much of the most powerful learning occurs, as John Dewey (1933) observed, through reflection on experience. What happens in the classroom can be a way to exponentially increase the impact of the experience through reflection, but we must remember that the experience itself is a vital prerequisite for the learning process.

- **Believe that there are a variety of ways to assess knowledge.** Because a functioning society requires that adults engage in a wide-ranging spectrum of careers, the end goal of education systems is not to create homogenized graduates who all share the exact same sets of skills and knowledge. And acknowledging such multiplicity means that we must also offer diverse ways for students to provide evidence of their learning processes and demonstrate the skills that they have acquired. Narrowly focused standardized tests fail to adequately account for the powerful diversity of knowledge and skills that position young people to thrive in today's changing and ever more complex world. We must move toward more holistic, competency-based methods of assessment that more effectively detect and celebrate the accomplishments of our students.

Ask yourself, "If I had the chance to do so today, how would I build a school system to meet the needs of all students, especially those furthest from opportunity?" Think of ways that your background or life experiences bring an underrepresented voice to this work. Reflect on the most significant leadership mistake you have made in your career and what you learned from that experience.

One way to change the context of learning in your school is to embrace the following core tenets of Leadership Soul:

- **Self-care.** Recognize that you are your own chief steward, and you must care for your spirit, your body, and your mind first.
- **Growth.** Do the work necessary to continue to evolve. Acquire knowledge, resources, and access. Expand your giving, influence, and compassion.
- **Intimacy.** Create safe spaces—trusted circles where you can be fully vulnerable. Give yourself permission to feel with abandon.
- **Purpose.** Focus on your impact. Do the little things with intent. Remember that the details truly do matter.

As previously mentioned, "leaving to learn" and real-world learning experiences are central to Big Picture Learning schools, and we have adopted the practice for aspiring leaders. We offer community-embedded experiences designed to highlight the leadership dispositions of community leaders as well as the opportunities and challenges they have encountered. "Leaving to learn" outings have included visits across the U.S.–Mexico border; to Ebenezer Baptist Church in Atlanta, Georgia; and to the Equal Justice Initiative's National Memorial for Peace and Justice and Legacy Museum in Montgomery, Alabama. These out-of-the-classroom learning experiences allow participants to gain new insight into leadership, reflect on what they have learned, and identify implications for their own work.

Embrace Love to Cultivate Relationships

If we accept the premise that the education system is designed to produce the results that we seek, then we must prioritize the most marginalized students, leaders, and communities. We must make the margin the new center of our attention. This will require a fundamental shift in understanding and mindset. The work of Leadership Soul entails culturally responsive school leadership, which Khalifa and colleagues (2016) argue must focus first on undoing oppressive forms of leadership that alienate and ostracize "minoritized" and marginalized students, invalidating their lived experiences in their homes, communities, and schools.

Here's a reflection from a leader connected to our network regarding her most significant leadership misstep and what she gained from that experience:

> I failed at relationship building. I just assumed we were all there to serve families and that alone was enough. It wasn't. I did not take time to build relationships with people above me or those on my team. I was all about the work, but no work can happen without the relationships to fuel the work. I knew that I was not "fitting in" and constantly felt outside of the staff. I knew I was doing something wrong but could not understand the "what" or "why" of it. I would later come to understand the significance of building "relational trust" to create and enable the conditions for organizational change to happen.

A leader who leads with love does the following:

- Fosters a positive and supportive learning environment by promoting trust, respect, and collaboration among students, staff, families, and community members.
- Develops stronger relationships with stakeholders, including students, staff, and families, which can lead to increased engagement and motivation.
- Promotes a growth mindset by encouraging students and staff to take risks and learn from their mistakes.
- Models empathy and understanding, creating a culture of inclusivity and diversity.
- Takes a holistic approach to leadership, considering the well-being of all stakeholders and working to address their needs.

One of the most important ways that school leaders can embrace love as the animating principle of their work is by creating a culture of positivity and respect. This involves using uplifting language, avoiding negative criticism, and recognizing and celebrating the unique strengths and abilities of each young person. Additionally, school leaders can create opportunities for students to feel valued and appreciated by regularly engaging in individual and group conversations with them, recognizing their achievements, and promoting their success.

Embracing love as a fundamental disposition also means investing in professional development and ongoing training for educators so they can better understand and address the unique needs and experiences of young people, especially those from marginalized communities. It is a transformative approach to education that has the potential for deep impact on the lives of young people.

On love and leadership, Nashville principal Brenda Diaz once again reflected:

> Love is not just this touchy-feely thing. It is strong. It is powerful. It is courageous. So, when you love, you love intensely. You are willing to go beyond yourself. The greatest love of all is to . . . literally lay

yourself down for someone else. Every day as a principal, I'm literally thinking of how I can lay myself down, not only for my students, but also for their families and for the teachers I serve. I am vulnerable enough to say that sometimes I don't always meet that mark.

I see Josue's, Angel's, and Shawn's stories differently now than when I was their advisor or school leader. The process of writing letters to them clarified that for me, even though I already knew that I had evolved as a leader—and as a human—since my early days with The Met. I was not the leader then that I am now—but I am also not yet fully the leader I aspire to be.

I have been blessed with outsized opportunities. My story as a young Afro-Latino man is both like and unlike that of many Black and Latino young men. Yes, I faced some trauma growing up, but my parents' extraordinary support undoubtedly made a difference in my journey. And my greatest blessings came when I first had the opportunity to work with youth at The Met—particularly the three young men who are at the center of this book. It's been one opportunity after another, one privilege after another.

I continue to draw heavily on my discussions with many members of my leadership network, particularly those in our Big Picture Learning schools and fellowships. Their voices help me make sense of my own journey and inspire and inform the journeys other leaders might take.

Conclusion

It is not our differences that divide us. It is our inability to recognize, accept, and celebrate those differences.

—Audre Lorde

It is our fundamental belief in the power of hope that has allowed us to rise above the voice of doubt and division, of anger and fear that we have faced in our own lives and in the life of this country. Our hope is that if we work hard enough and believe in ourselves, then we can be whatever we dream regardless of the limitations that others may place on us. The hope that when people see us for who we truly are, maybe, just maybe, they too will be inspired to rise to their best possible selves.

—Michelle Obama

A Big Picture Learning network school leader captured the essence of the challenges we face as follows: "It's trying to build a culture so that we can create new expectations for ourselves." That culture is central to cultivating new forms of leadership that are essential to serving students and their families, community members, and educators. But I recognize that the process is ever-evolving.

Leadership Soul is about leading from the soul rather than going through the technical motions. Principal Shavonne McMillan of Vaux High School in Philadelphia shared how that looks in her work:

> I've cried in front of the staff. I've been angry in front of staff and students. Because I want them to know it's a safe space to bring their whole authentic selves. I think that's when we can do our best work, and we can then model that for kids.

To attain our loftiest goals, the technical competencies so essential to leadership—developing strategies, thinking and behaving systemically, engaging the community, supporting staff—must be balanced by leading with and through love, care, and vulnerability.

Lead with Love

I hope that I've shared the vital importance of demonstrating love in classrooms and schools. The guiding principles I want you to take away from this book in that regard include the following:

- Create a supportive and inclusive learning environment where all students feel valued and respected, regardless of their background, abilities, and cultural identities.
- Provide individualized attention to students who need it, taking the time to listen to their concerns and helping them overcome challenges, explore their interests, and pursue opportunities.
- Encourage students to take risks and to embrace their individuality by fostering a culture of creativity and experimentation.
- Celebrate students' successes and recognize their achievements by creating opportunities for them to share their work with their classmates and to receive positive feedback from peers and teachers.
- Build strong relationships with students and families, getting to know them as individuals and learning about their unique needs and experiences.

- Provide ongoing professional development opportunities for staff to ensure they have the skills and knowledge necessary to support students and create a positive school environment.
- Encourage teamwork among staff and students by creating opportunities for them to collaborate and develop their leadership skills.
- Foster a culture of kindness and respect by promoting positive behavior and avoiding negative criticism or bullying.

"Love slows us down," observed a Big Picture Learning principal about Leadership Soul and her work. "Love makes us see one another and make connections." Here's how young people across schools in the Big Picture Learning network have responded to the love their school leaders and teachers have demonstrated to them (quotes are from interviews conducted in July 2022):

- Increased engagement and motivation in learning: "I feel like my advisor/teacher really cares about me and my success. It motivates me to work harder in class."
- Improved behavior and relationships: "I used to get into a lot of trouble in school, but my principal showed me that he cared and believed in me. Now, I want to do better and make him proud."
- Increased sense of belonging: "My advisor/teacher makes me feel like I'm part of the class, and she always takes time to listen to me and understand where I'm coming from. Because of [her], I can say that I'll be able to navigate these (next) four years of my life not feeling alone."
- Greater self-esteem and confidence: "My principal always tells me that I'm smart and capable. It makes me feel good about myself and helps me believe in my abilities."
- A desire to give back: "I appreciate everything my advisor/teacher has done for me. I want to pay it forward and help others the way he has helped me."

Lead with Care

Leading with care is crucial, particularly in schools that serve our most marginalized and vulnerable youth. Prioritizing care in our leadership approach creates a safe and nurturing environment where students feel valued, supported, and understood. Educators who lead with care can help students find solutions to their challenges and create opportunities for positive outcomes.

Students who feel cared for are more likely to develop a sense of belonging and trust in adults and peers. This emotional connection also enhances their overall well-being, resilience, and motivation to learn. Educators who maintain caring relationships with their students understand their unique circumstance and diverse needs, and thus are better positioned to provide personalized support such as trauma-informed practices, culturally responsive teaching, and individualized interventions.

School leaders who focus on care and establish a supportive working environment reap the benefits of an organizational culture that fosters collaboration, professional growth, and collective efficacy among staff members. This, in turn, enhances the overall quality of students' educational experiences and strengthens the school's ability to meet the needs of its marginalized students.

To incorporate care into your daily practices, start by actively listening to your students and demonstrating empathy toward their experiences and challenges. This involves creating a safe and non-judgmental space where students feel comfortable sharing their thoughts and emotions. Prioritize building strong relationships with your students, taking the time to understand their individual strengths, interests, and needs.

Another important aspect of leading with care is being responsive to students' social and emotional well-being. Consider establishing regular check-in times, such as morning meetings or advisory periods, where students have an opportunity to express their feelings and discuss any concerns. Create a supportive classroom community through activities like team-building exercises, cooperative learning, and peer mentoring to foster care and collaboration among students.

Educators who lead with care exhibit compassion, patience, and understanding. They approach their work with a genuine commitment to the holistic development of their students, valuing their individuality and cultural backgrounds. They are attentive to signs of distress or trauma and seek appropriate support systems or resources to address these issues. Additionally, educators who lead with care are reflective practitioners, continually seeking to improve their own practice and staying informed about best practices in social-emotional learning and trauma-informed education.

Lead with Vulnerability

Leadership Soul encompasses an acceptance of mutual interdependence. It is about what we owe one another and the commitment we want to make to one another. We cannot lead students if we do not love them or care for them or are not open to them.

It is vulnerability that will help leaders break down the isolation that preceded and has been exacerbated by the COVID-19 pandemic, and it is vulnerability that will help leaders give up their inclination toward control and top-down directive formal authority. Not only is control ineffective, but it is also debilitating and diminishes engagement, agency, and responsibility.

As Christopher Emdin observed in his keynote address at Big Bang 2022, Big Picture Learning's annual summer conference:

> You can either close the door to possibilities and let folks wax poetic in the language of their dysfunction, or usher them into the new possibilities. It is easy to stand at the door and profess the language. It is hard to unlock the door and let folks in.

Vulnerability means that we are available, accessible, constantly listening, and open to learning. Giving up control and embracing Leadership Soul means avoiding grouping, labeling, and tracking young people. Labels and groups create distance and contribute to a loss of understanding. Once you label, you forget the individual.

It takes courage to deliberately place yourself in vulnerable situations or relationships—courage to become intentionally, conscientiously vulnerable in order to strengthen relationships, to embrace your Leadership Soul. Vulnerability entails trust, which is a function of competence and caring. As one Big Picture Learning network leader observed, "I have to be able to know myself. I have to be able to love myself. And if I can do those things, I can be a leader who wants that of others." Vulnerability goes beyond the passive "My door is always open."

Here is an example from one of our schools. Mr. Johnson was a high school teacher who always emphasized the importance of caring and vulnerability in his work and interactions with students. One student in particular, Trae, a young, male student of color, was struggling and feeling disconnected from school.

Mr. Johnson took a special interest in Trae and made it a priority to build a relationship with him based on care and trust. He made time to meet with Trae regularly and listen to his concerns, showing genuine interest in his life outside school. He made time to connect with his family members and reach out to them whenever Trae was making progress and to gain some insight into Trae's personality and home life.

One day, Trae confided in Mr. Johnson that he was struggling with feelings of isolation and anger, due in part to challenges he was facing at home. Mr. Johnson showed vulnerability by sharing his own experiences with similar challenges, allowing Trae to feel heard and understood. Together, and with the consent of Trae's family, they sought out some counseling and a variety of positive outlets for Trae.

Mr. Johnson and Trae worked jointly on strategies to help Trae manage his emotions and stay focused on his goals. Through this process, Mr. Johnson emphasized the importance of caring for oneself and seeking support when needed. As a result of Mr. Johnson's approach, Trae began to feel more connected to school and saw a significant improvement in his engagement, his learning, and his overall well-being.

The Heart of Leadership Soul

Leadership Soul gets to the core of who and what we are all about. This type of leadership requires high levels of competence and commitment to get right. Here again is Chris Emdin (2022):

> Your mind has a finite capacity to soak in information. But if I speak to your soul, there's a miracle that happens where the capacity of the mind to contain the fullness of the information gets expanded exponentially. It takes courage to make this shift public. Oftentimes, it feels like swimming upstream. But if you know something and you believe something in your heart—in your spirit—things can be inherently different.

Leadership Soul is a spiritual thing. It's the invisible inner being of servant leaders—those who typically lead from the side to raise up the Leadership Soul of others—that becomes visible when we act selflessly. Call it spirit, essence, or source; it is the force behind our thoughts, words, and actions. Leaders who lead with their souls understand and tap into this "inner voice" to manifest their vision and values.

As principals or system leaders, we each hold a vision for schools that is elegantly intertwined with our values, our dreams, and our desires for our community and our world. We understand that every school is part of a larger, more complex ecology that both shapes it and is shaped by it. We are conscious of the impact of our choices and decisions not just on ourselves but on everyone who is close to us.

Leadership Soul demands that leaders show up with their whole being, not just their highly polished and credentialed selves. They leave their qualifications at the door. Leaders with soul don't claim to have all the answers. They can admit that they are flawed and will make mistakes. They use the language of this book without citing it specifically. They speak of love, care, and vulnerability, even without applying a formal framework. Leadership Soul is in their core; it just needs to be brought to the surface.

From the Margins to the Center

Leadership Soul is not exclusively the domain of people of color. Leaders with soul recognize the many forms of privilege that shape who they are and how they go about their leadership. We need to fundamentally change our educational worldview to shift those on the margins to the center. In far too many cases, the current conventional approach to schooling is designed to sort and marginalize, isolating and silencing voices that need to be heard. Leadership Soul cannot flourish in such settings.

We must strive for simultaneous primacy of the individual and the group, the uniqueness of each person and the agency we know they possess. When we honor and value individual students, we relieve them from the pressures of conformity to a "standard" that does not account for their lived experiences. Greg Lucas, director of social and emotional learning at New Visions for Public Schools and a member of Big Picture Learning's Deep Learning Equity Fellowship, commented on how conventional schools too frequently treat marginalized students:

> It's really a stripping away of who [boys of color] are. You know, let's take 'em on a retreat and tell 'em how to tie ties and tell 'em not to wear a durag. We are essentially telling them, "We need you to understand. This world will not make space for who you are as you are. You won't really ever belong, but I can get you to a place where you can at least fit in." Are we going to be complicit with helping to strip them away further? Or are we going to help them announce themselves to the world?

Leadership Soul matters more now than ever; it isn't an abstract vision that only exists in some far-off hypothetical future. It's where you come from each day. It's how you think and how you act. Leading with soul means making an intentional effort to make changes now that bring the future into the present. I call upon all allies, partners, graduates, and students to move beyond searching their hearts, beyond thoughts and prayers, beyond heartfelt social media posts to embrace the work of Leadership Soul.

Through Leadership Soul, we move not to rebuild but to reset. We will not accept a new normal. We will reject the comfort of the recent past. And we will not build upon any promise of a future that does not also dismantle the oppressive policies and practices that brought us to the precipice upon which we currently stand.

It is Big Picture Learning's vision—as it should be for all who possess or aspire to possess Leadership Soul—that all young people, all humans, can live and *deserve* to live lives of their own design, supported by a caring society and given equitable opportunities to achieve their greatest potential. We must move forward prepared to activate the power of our communities for justice. For dignity. For respect. For good.

Postscript

I believe that some degree of Leadership Soul has always directed my practice, but I also feel that I was unable to fully tap into it during the years that I had the great privilege to mentor and learn alongside Josue, Angel, and Shawn. This is why the letters I've shared—actual letters I sent—are filled as much with regret as they are with love. Back then, I didn't know what I didn't know. I still don't know what I don't know, but I know that I know *more* now. The lessons I've learned through developing my Leadership Soul—through my experiences with these amazing young men—give me hope that we can all guide young people in new ways that fully embrace and reflect love, care, and vulnerability.

The letters you've read thus far in this book focus on what young people needed from me as they attempted to make their way in the world and achieve whatever success looked like for them. Those letters show how an array of forces led to insurmountable challenges that needed heavy doses of love, caring, and vulnerability.

I close out this book with two more letters.

One is to another young man of color, Michael Walters, an alumnus of Fannie Lou Hamer Freedom High School in the Bronx, part of the Big Picture Learning network of schools. When I met Michael, he was nearing graduation and had been offered a college scholarship as well as an award from the Garden of Dreams Foundation at a ceremony at Madison Square Garden. After watching a video of Michael's speech at that ceremony, I knew that Michael's story was worth sharing as an exemplar—an image of potentiality—that would help others understand how many of our young people overcome truly challenging circumstances to achieve their ambitious visions for themselves. In my letter to Michael, I have tried to share some of what I learned from him and the positive impact that his school community had on him.

The other letter is to my daughter Bella, whom I've alluded to several times in this book. This letter focuses on the future and the promises that educators and everyone in the community need to make to all young people. I believe in and work toward this vision every day of my life. I hope you will join me—join us—on the journey.

To Michael Walters

Dear Michael,

I am so pleased to learn that you have graduated from Fannie Lou Hamer Freedom High School (in my hometown of the Bronx!) and are going off to college soon. You may be the first in your family to do so, but you are one in a long line of Black and Brown young men who have achieved outsize success despite enormous challenges. Like so many of our brilliant young brothers, you've witnessed a lot—at home and in the streets—and you've had adults around who would move heaven and earth to provide you with shelter, safety, love, and opportunity.

Abuse, poverty, fear, and frequent dislocation were often part of your daily experience. You spoke of living in a domestic violence shelter during the last four years, protected from the violence you observed in the streets. I am saddened to learn that the shelter may continue to serve as your home even as you pursue your degree.

The challenges you have endured and overcome are almost beyond my ability to grasp. It was heart-wrenching to hear about what you have endured on your way to graduation and to the start of a college program that will lead you to your goal of a degree in social work. I do not doubt your own childhood experiences have motivated your career choice.

Amid these threats to your well-being, you found another kind of shelter in your school. Over the last four years, Fannie Lou Hamer Freedom High School has provided you with an opportunity to rejuvenate your learning and supported you in preparing yourself for all the learning and work ahead.

Of course, Fannie Lou could not protect you from the lockdowns and isolation forced on you by COVID-19. Remote learning from the shelter was yet another challenge you overcame.

You and your generation of learners have inherited far too many broken and battered systems. Many have not fared well. I fear that could have been your fate as well were it not for your loving mom, who bravely moved with you to the Bronx and enrolled you at Fannie Lou.

Our country's response to the COVID-19 pandemic—lockdowns, isolation, masks, vaccination mandates—wreaked havoc on your learning. You lost considerable time, but hopefully not opportunity. The system was broken long before the pandemic, and I suspect progress in its aftermath will be meager without more fundamental changes to the toxic cultures, systems, and structures in which the forces of marginalization take root.

For many of your peers, their potential was diminished not only by the pandemic but also by deliberate marginalization. Many young people have not been—and, sadly, will not be—as resilient as you. Young people have lost control of their education to adults who do not know them.

As much as you have overcome and as much as you have accomplished—as much love, care, and vulnerability as you have experienced—the challenges will persist. You now need to find at college the supportive environment, learning community, and family you found at your beloved Fannie Lou.

As a parent, the love and protection you have received from your mom resonates deeply with me. My Leadership Soul is strengthened by learning from you and your story.

I am moved by your advice to your peers: "Understand that this is a small part of our lives, and we must grasp and know within ourselves that there is more to our stories."

I am even more enormously moved and touched by your advice to me and others pursuing their Leadership Soul:

Be willing to give "gems" and realize that even if it may seem like we're not paying attention, don't stop. We hear them. We use them. Don't underestimate what young people are going through and dealing with. Seek to understand. Share love. Show that you care. Continue to create spaces that allow us to be vulnerable. Then, be prepared for what you might hear. We will push and challenge. Know that it's not personal. Don't back down from our rage.

It seems that everything is increasingly fragile, on the edge of breaking down—people, systems, communities, families. And yet, as fragile as our systems and structures may be, they endure, though corrupted by toxic policies, protocols, and practices. Fragility entails fear and anxiety. Tranquility seems forever just beyond reach.

To help you escape this corrupted ecology and forge a way forward, your school chose to work around, over, and through that toxic mix. These efforts required uncommon leadership—Leadership Soul, which I believe points the way toward creating a total learner experience that challenges the systems of marginalization that are embedded in the culture, systems, structures, and practices of the entire education system.

I am looking for positive steps forward—for the roses that continue to grow up from the cracks in the concrete. And I am grateful to have found so many blossoms in your story.

I will continue to help bring young people who have been pushed to the margins back to the center. I will continue to work with my colleagues to create opportunities for you and future generations to show what you know and can do in more authentic ways. I will continue to help you hone your own Leadership Soul and exhibit love, care, and vulnerability toward your peers, your family, and your community.

Love is at the core of everything. It enables caring and allows for vulnerability. It provides the context in which trusting relationships can be formed. I cannot lead you if I do not love you, if I do not care for you, and if I am not open to you.

Leadership Soul reaffirms the primacy of each and every individual learner. The system needs champions who will treat marginalized individuals and their priorities with love and care. To accomplish that, we need a radical reset in our relationships with young people and their families.

Young people need to experience love, care, and vulnerability in order to practice love, care, and vulnerability as adults and leaders in their homes, workplaces, and communities.

As Neil Postman once observed, "Children are the living messages we send to a time we will not see." I can think of no better statement to convey to you the enormity of the responsibility I and all leaders have to young Black and Brown men.

How will we prepare you to flourish in your future? What promises will I, as a developing leader with soul, make to you? Here's a starter set.

I will embrace Leadership Soul as the driving force of my true authentic self as a leader. I will be more public with my Leadership Soul. This requires a commitment to decentering myself from the learning of young people and prioritizing each student and their needs above everything else.

I will approach all students (especially those who have historically been kept furthest from quality opportunities) with an ethic of care, love, and vulnerability. Leading with love, care, and vulnerability isn't soft. It requires building enough capital with each young person for there to be an honest and trusting relationship.

I will provide learners with unfettered access to an abundance of learning opportunities and environments to prepare them for their journey.

I will encourage more Black and Brown students to consider becoming educators in formal and informal ways. I will openly discuss the beauty and challenges that come along with this work.

I will recognize and celebrate how unique each young person is and how worthy they are of a truly personalized set of learning opportunities.

I will work with you and your family to support your own emerging development as a leader with soul.

My hope is that fulfilling these promises will help you and your generation to realize all that you want. I have a dream that an unburdened generation of young people who see themselves at the margins will rise and claim their rightful place at the center.

Michael, you are an exemplification of Leadership Soul and of the love, care, and vulnerability I wish for all leaders in our schools. You have helped me to see the potential of Leadership Soul. The future is bright because it is in your hands.

Stay up, Young King,

Carlos

To Isabella Moreno

You rose into my life like a promised sunrise, brightening my days with the light in your eyes. I've never been so strong. Now I'm where I belong.

—Maya Angelou

Bella,

I am up before dawn gazing at the fading stars, and thoughts of you prompted me to write this letter. I cherish this opportunity to reflect on where I am on my journey as a leader and as the father of the most inspiring human I've ever met. I can think of no better way to conclude my most important piece of writing.

These last few years of the pandemic proved to be chiflado (crazy)! And the last few months have been especially difficult and challenging. I know that spending some of your high school years in quarantine and hybrid learning is not what you had hoped for or expected.

Being quarantined for so long completely changed the way that I think about time. I often lost track of what day or even week it was. But I'm eternally grateful for and appreciative of how much more time we had to spend together.

Tonight, I find myself thinking about the future—your future. I have this image of you preparing to leave home for college, off to Duke to join the rowing team. Mommy and I are so very proud and happy! Although I'm nervous about you leaving, I know that you are ready. You'll be fine. In fact, you'll be better than fine!

You are brilliant, kind, compassionate, and just. You received an education that focused on learning and not just test scores from a public school with resources for everything you needed, from a rigorous and engaging curriculum to Black and Brown teachers who represented the diversity of your community. You are a reflection of what our country can be and what it needs. You are a natural leader and protector of those who need the greatest protection! The world will be a better place because of you. I'm reminded of young women like you—women such as

Malala Yousafzai, Amanda Gorman, and Greta Thunberg—who have demonstrated that young people can make a difference. You are everything that we need!

Did I ever share with you that some people wanted us to name you Milagros instead of Isabella? Milagros is Spanish for "miracle." You entered this world 4 months early, weighing less than 2 pounds—but "miracle" would refer only to your birth, not your life. You are a fighter. You have always been strong in every way. You possess intelligence, beauty, and compassion. Isabella means "beautiful," and you inherited the empathy and strength that Grandma Isabel, your namesake, carried until the age of 98. I pray your life is as long and as rich as hers was.

The real miracle was the relentless love, patience, and compassion consistently demonstrated by the nursing staff at Women & Infants Hospital in Providence. The care and attention they showed you, me, and Mommy was truly miraculous. They stayed alongside us on rough nights when your oxygen levels were dangerously low and celebrated your growth and progress. They modeled the ethos of patience, encouragement, vulnerability, and love that we needed to see and feel as new parents. We learned to be better parents because of them.

I think of the nursing staff often as a dad, but even more as an educator. All that they did for us when our family was most vulnerable influenced the way I try to show up inside classrooms and schools. I try to carry this ethos in all my work.

I could not have been prouder to see you take to the streets of our town in May 2020, wearing a mask, to express your outrage at George Floyd's murder and to exclaim with pain-filled passion that Black Lives Matter. It was one of my proudest moments, watching you lead thousands of young people and adults in a march for some of our most basic human rights. You have known from a young age that "freedom is never voluntarily given by the oppressor. It must be demanded by the oppressed!" Martin Luther King Jr.'s inspirational words ring out through your actions.

Bella, you've seen how I struggled looking back on my relationships with the three young men I've profiled in my book. You're my child, but they were also part of my family. From them, I learned lessons filled with pain and hurt that I pray you won't have to experience. You can lead differently and better. You can be more loving, caring, and vulnerable. You can and must make a difference. I know you will be a leader with soul. In many ways, you already are.

A leader I know recently shared with me, "Love slows us down to observe more carefully and creates new ways of being with one another." This is a kind of love many marginalized youth never experience. Still, there is no single movement in the history of this world that did not have young people at its forefront. Bring others to this quest for Leadership Soul. Practice and model love, care, and vulnerability.

The system needs champions who provide love and care for individuals and groups on the margins. I am confident that you and your peers can turn the tide for the new generation of leaders with soul. As I observe the state of our democracy, it is clear to me that we need new and better ways going forward. Major institutions are failing due to a lack of leadership, resources, and honesty. This is what keeps me up at night. ¡Chiflado!

We adults have work to do. Far too much of current leadership is rooted in intellect and selfishness, not soul. To overcome this state of affairs, leaders—including mothers and fathers—must focus on love, care, and vulnerability. I am committed to doing my part. But eventually, we have to get out of the way, pass the reins, and let the soul of the youth take the lead. The world needs you to fully realize the beautiful and amazing changemaker that you are destined to be!

I will end here for now, baby girl. The sun is beginning to rise. It's a new day.

Love you,

Dad

Acknowledgments

As I reflect upon the journey that led to the creation of this book—a journey that began as an idea on August 30, 2018—my heart swells with gratitude for the many people who have played an instrumental role in bringing this vision to life. I am profoundly thankful for the diverse tapestry of individuals who have contributed their time, insights, and unwavering support.

First, I would like to extend a heartfelt thank-you to the families of the young people whose stories are featured in this book, including Rosa Morales, Julie White Gooding, Sabrina Pao, and Michael Walters. Thank you for sharing details about yourselves and your loved ones' journeys, struggles, and triumphs. Your openness has not only grounded this text but also provided a profound reminder of the impact that young people can have on adults—when we allow ourselves to listen. I am honored to have known them all.

I would also like to offer my deep gratitude to my SQUAD: Dr. Fawziah Qadir, Dr. Charmaine Mercer, Dr. Monica White, Chris Jackson, Charlie Mojkowski, y mi hermano Andrew Frishman. You have helped to breathe life into these pages with your critical honesty, imaginative thinking, and artistic perspectives. Your ability to see beyond the ordinary and willingness to ride with me to create something grounded in truth and beauty has been the cornerstone of this work. You have helped ensure that the ideas presented here are rooted in scholarly rigor, practical wisdom, and soul. I am truly grateful for your dedication to making this work shine.

To my Big Picture Learning national team and network of school leaders, who inspire me daily: you are the living embodiment of Leadership Soul. Your commitment to fostering positive change, your resilience in the face of challenges, and your unwavering dedication to uplifting young people and those around you have been a constant source of inspiration. Your stories have breathed life into the concepts explored in this book, reminding us of the transformative power of authentic leadership.

A special acknowledgment to the Ashé and Equity Fellows family and all the amazing Leadership Journeys alumni, whose wisdom and insights have deeply enriched the conversations within these pages: your commitment to living, learning, and leading publicly have affirmed my beliefs and expanded my thinking. The dialogue and moments we've shared have been invaluable, and I am honored to learn alongside you all.

Of those who have shared their stories and their time—all of whom I have deep admiration for—I'd like to explicitly thank my brother Dr. Christopher Emdin. From day one, you said this book needed to be written, and your check-ins on its progress helped to keep me honest and on track. Thank you, and here's to continuing to "stay low and keep firing!"

Lastly, to Quay and Bella: your unwavering support, love, understanding, and patience throughout this five-year journey cannot be measured. Your love has fueled my determination, and your belief in me has propelled me forward, even when the path seemed daunting. Thank you for your faith in me and in this book!

   This book is a testament to the power of possibility and the beauty of leading with *love, care,* and *vulnerability.* To all those who have played a part, no matter how big or small, in the creation of this work, I extend my deepest and most heartfelt gratitude. May the ideas within these pages continue to inspire and guide, just as you all have inspired and guided me.

Los

References

Alder, N. (2002). Interpretations of the meaning of care: Creating caring relationships in urban middle school classrooms. *Urban Education, 37*(2), 241–266.

Anderson, G. L. (1990). Toward a critical constructivist approach to school administration: Invisibility, legitimation, and the study of non-events. *Educational Administration Quarterly, 26*(1), 38–59.

Banda, R., Reyes, G., & Caldas, B. (2020). Curricula of care and radical love. *Oxford Research Encyclopedias.* doi:10.1093/acrefore/9780190264093.013.1434

Bass, L. (2012). When care trumps justice: The operationalization of Black feminist caring in educational leadership. *International Journal of Qualitative Studies in Education, 25*(1), 73–87.

Bass, L. R. (2020). Black male leaders care too: An introduction to Black masculine caring in educational leadership. *Educational Administration Quarterly, 56*(3), 353–395.

Bass, L., & Alston, K. (2018). Black masculine caring and the dilemma faced by Black male leaders. *Journal of School Leadership, 28*(6), 772–787.

Bond, M. J., & Herman, A. A. (2016). Lagging life expectancy for Black men: A public health imperative. *American Journal of Public Health, 106*(7), 1167–1169. https://www.ncbi.nlm.nih.gov/pmc/articles/PMC4984780/

Brantmeier, E. J. (2013). Pedagogy of vulnerability: Definitions, assumptions, and applications. In J. Lin, R. Oxford, & E. J. Brantmeier (Eds.), *Re-envisioning higher education: Embodied pathways to wisdom and transformation* (pp. 95–106). Information Age Publishing.

Brockenbrough, E. (2015). "The discipline stop": Black male teachers and the politics of urban school discipline. *Education and Urban Society, 47*(5), 499–522.

Brown, B. (2018). *Dare to lead: Brave work. Tough conversations. Whole hearts.* Random House.

Burton, L. (2007). Childhood adultification in economically disadvantaged families: A conceptual model. *Family Relations, 56*(4), 329–345.

Byrne-Jiménez, M. C., & Yoon, I. H. (2019). Leadership as an act of love: Leading in dangerous times. *Frontiers in Education, 3.* doi:10.3389/feduc.2018.00117

Callahan, A. (2020, June 10). *Why Black male teachers matter.* American Federation of Teachers. https://www.aft.org/news/why-black-male-teachers -matter

Collins, P. H. (1989). The social construction of Black feminist thought. *Signs: Journal of Women in Culture and Society, 14*(4), 745–773.

Collins, P. H. (2002). *Black feminist thought: Knowledge, consciousness, and the politics of empowerment.* Routledge.

Cross, N. (2020). What's going right? Language play and bilingual identities in a predominantly African American dual-language classroom. *Penn GSE Perspectives on Urban Education, 17.* https://urbanedjournal.gse.upenn.edu /volume-17-spring-2020/what%E2%80%99s-going-right-language-play-and -bilingual-identities-predominantly

Dancy, T. E. (2014). The adultification of Black Boys. In K. J. Fasching-Varner, R. E. Reynolds, K. A. Albert, & L. L. Martin (Eds.), *Trayvon Martin, race, and American justice: Writing wrong* (vol. 1, pp. 49–56). Sense Publishers.

Daniels, E. A. (2012). *Fighting, loving, teaching: An exploration of hope, armed love and critical urban pedagogies.* Sense Publishers.

Dantley, M. E. (2009). African American educational leadership: Critical, purposive, and spiritual. In L. Foster & L. C. Tillman (Eds.), *African American perspectives on leadership in schools: Building a culture of empowerment* (pp. 39–56). Rowman & Littlefield Education.

Delpit, L. (2006). *Other people's children: Cultural conflict in the classroom.* New Press.

Dewey, J. (1933). *How we think: A restatement of the relation of reflective thinking to the educative process.* D. C. Health.

Diaz, R. (2011). Historical images of Puerto Ricans: The case of the South Bronx. *Transforming Anthropology, 19*(1), 53–57.

DoSomething.org. (2023). *11 facts about high school dropout rates.* https:// www.dosomething.org/us/facts/11-facts-about-high-school-dropout-rates

Duncan-Andrade, J. (2009). Note to educators: Hope required when growing roses in concrete. *Harvard Educational Review, 79*(2), 181–194.

Egalite, A. J., Kisida, B., & Winters, M. A. (2015). Representation in the classroom: The effect of own-race teachers on student achievement. *Economics of Education Review, 45,* 44–52.

Emdin, C. (2022). *Keynote address.* Big Picture Learning Annual Summer Conference, Hollywood, FL.

Engle, J., & Tinto, V. (2008). *Moving beyond access: College success for low-income, first-generation students.* Pell Institute for the Study of Opportunity in Higher Education.

Estrada, P. (2014). English learner curricular streams in four middle schools: Triage in the trenches. *The Urban Review, 46*(4), 535–573.

Fergus, A. (2010). *Bad boys: Public schools in the making of Black masculinity.* University of Michigan Press.

Freire, P. (1985). *The politics of education: Culture, power, and liberation.* Greenwood.

Friedman-Krauss, A. H., Barnett, W. S., Hodges, K. S, Weisenfeld, G. G., Gardiner, B., & Jost, T. M. (2022). *The state of preschool 2021: State preschool yearbook.* National Institute for Early Education Research, Rutgers University. https://nieer.org/wp-content/uploads/2022/09/YB2021_Full_Report.pdf

Gandara, P., Rumberger, R., Maxwell-Jolly, J., & Callahan, R. (2003). English learners in California schools: Unequal resources, unequal outcomes. *Education Policy Analysis Archives, 11,* 36.

Ginwright, S. (2006). Racial justice through resistance: Important dimensions of youth development for African Americans. *National Civic Review, 95*(1), 41–46.

Gonzalez, E. (2004). *The Bronx.* Columbia University Press.

Greene, M. (1978). Teaching: The personal reality. *Teachers College Record, 80*(1), 24–35. doi:10.1177/016146817808000102

Guinier, L. (2016). *The tyranny of the meritocracy: Democratizing higher education in America.* Penguin Random House.

Gutiérrez, K. D., & Orellana, M. F. (2006). At last: The "problem" of English learners: Constructing genres of difference. *Research in the Teaching of English, 40*(4), 502–507.

Heiser, C. A., Prince, K., & Levy, J. D. (2017). Examining critical theory as a framework to advance equity through student affairs assessment. *Journal of Student Affairs Inquiry, 2*(1), 1–17.

hooks, b. (1994) *Teaching to transgress: Education as the practice of freedom.* Routledge.

Hoyle, J. R., & Slater, R. O. (2001). Love, happiness, and America's schools: The role of educational leadership in the 21st century. *Phi Delta Kappan, 82*(10), 790–794.

Hurtado, A., Haney, C. W., & Hurtado, J. G. (2012). "Where the boys are": Macro and micro considerations for the study of young Latino men's educational achievement. In P. A. Noguera, A. Hurtado, & E. Fergus (Eds.), *Invisible no more: Understanding the disenfranchisement of Latino men and boys* (pp. 101–121). Taylor & Francis Group.

Jackson, I., Sealey-Ruiz, Y., & Watson, W. (2014). Reciprocal love: Mentoring Black and Latino males through an ethos of care. *Urban Education, 49*(4), 394–417.

Kanno, Y., & Kangas, S. E. (2014). "I'm not going to be, like, for the AP": English language learners' limited access to advanced college-preparatory courses in high school. *American Educational Research Journal, 51*(5), 848–878.

Khalifa, M. A., Gooden, M. A., & Davis, J. E. (2016). Culturally responsive school leadership: A synthesis of the literature. *Review of Educational Research, 86*(4), 1272–1311.

Kwenda, C. V. (2003). Cultural justice: The pathway to reconciliation and social cohesion. In D. Chidester, P. Dexter, & W. James (Eds.), *What holds us together: Social cohesion in South Africa* (pp. 67–80). HSRC Press.

Ladson-Billings, G. (2006). From the achievement gap to the education debt: Understanding achievement in U.S. schools. *Educational Researcher, 35*(7), 3–12.

Larson, C. L., & Murtadha, K. (2002). Leadership for social justice. *Teachers College Record, 104*(9), 134–161.

Love, B. L. (2019). *We want to do more than survive: Abolitionist teaching and the pursuit of educational freedom.* Beacon Press.

Mahler, J. (2006). *Ladies and gentlemen, the Bronx is burning: 1977, baseball, politics, and the battle for the soul of a city.* Macmillan.

Maslow, A. H. (1963). The need to know and the fear of knowing. *Journal of General Psychology, 68*(1), 111–125. doi:10.1080/00221309.1963.9920516

Menakem, R. (2017). *My grandmother's hands: Racialized trauma and the pathway to mending our hearts and bodies.* Central Recovery Press.

Miller, P. M., Brown, T., & Hopson, R. (2011). Centering love, hope, and trust in the community: Transformative urban leadership informed by Paulo Freire. *Urban Education, 46*(5), 1078–1099.

Murtadha, K., & Watts, D. M. (2005). Linking the struggle for education and social justice: Historical perspectives of African American leadership in schools. *Educational Administration Quarterly, 41*(4), 591–608.

National Center for Education Statistics (NCES). (2023, May). Racial/ethnic enrollment in public schools. *Condition of education.* U.S. Department of Education, Institute of Education Sciences. https://nces.ed.gov/programs/coe/indicator/cge/racial-ethnic-enrollment

National Partnership for Women & Families. (2018). *Listening to Latina mothers in California*. https://www.nationalpartnership.org/our-work/resources /health-care/maternity/listening-to-latina-mothers-in-california.pdf

Noddings, N. (1984). *Caring: A feminine approach to ethics and moral education*. University of California Press.

Noddings, N. (2002). *Educating moral people: A caring alternative to character education*. Teachers College Press.

Noddings, N. (2005). *The challenge to care in schools* (2nd ed.). Teachers College Press.

Noddings, N. (2013). An ethic of caring. In R. Shafer-Landau (Ed.), *Ethical theory: An anthology* (2nd ed., pp. 699–712). Wiley-Blackwell.

Noguera, P. A. (2012). Saving Black and Latino boys: What schools can do to make a difference. *Phi Delta Kappan, 93*(5), 8–12.

Noguera, P., Hurtado, A., & Fergus, E. (Eds.). (2012). *Invisible no more: Understanding the disenfranchisement of Latino men and boys*. Routledge.

Orfield, G., Kuscera, J., & Siegel-Hawley, G. (2012). *E pluribus . . . separation: Deepening double segregation for more students*. Civil Rights Project UCLA.

P, K. (2020, December 5). *23 college dropout statistics that will surprise you*. CreditDonkey. https://www.creditdonkey.com/college-dropout-statistics .html

Rhode Island KIDS COUNT. (2020). *New census data shows: Rhode Island ranked 21st in child poverty*. https://www.rikidscount.org/Portals/0/Uploads /Documents/Media%20Releases/9.17.20%20Media%20Release%20 -%20Child%20Poverty_2019%20-%20final.pdf

Ricciulli, V. (2019, May 3). *In the 1970s, the Bronx was burning, but some residents were rebuilding*. Curbed New York. https://ny.curbed.com/2019/5/3 /18525908/south-bronx-fires-decade-of-fire-vivian-vazquez-documentary

Rivera-McCutchen, R. L. (2012). Caring in a small urban high school: A complicated success. *Urban Education, 47*(3), 653–680.

Rivera-McCutchen, R. L. (2019). Armed love in school leadership: Resisting inequality and injustice in schooling. *Leadership and Policy in Schools, 18*(2), 237–247.

Schein, E., & Schein, P. (2018). *Humble leadership: The power of relationships, openness, and trust* (Kindle ed.). Berrett-Koehler.

Schott Foundation for Public Education. (2015). *Black lives matter: The Schott 50 state report on public education and Black males*. https://schottfoundation .org/wp-content/uploads/blacklivesmatter2015_0.pdf

Sen, A. (2011). *Development as freedom*. Knopf Doubleday.

Siddle Walker, V., & Snarey, J. R. (Eds.). (2004). *Race-ing moral formation: African American perspectives on care and justice*. Teachers College Press.

Sizer, T. R. (2004). *Horace's compromise: The dilemma of the American high school: With a new preface.* Houghton Mifflin Harcourt.

Sizer, T. R. (2009). *I cannot teach a child I do not know.* Speech delivered at the Australian National Schools Network.

Strongin, F. F. V. (2017). *"You don't have a problem, until you do": Revitalization and gentrification in Providence, Rhode Island* (Doctoral dissertation, Massachusetts Institute of Technology).

Taylor, J. K. (2020). Structural racism and maternal health among Black women. *The Journal of Law, Medicine & Ethics, 48*(3), 506–517.

Umansky, I. M., & Dumont, H. (2021). English learner labeling: How English learner classification in kindergarten shapes teacher perceptions of student skills and the moderating role of bilingual instructional settings. *American Educational Research Journal, 58*(5), 993–1031.

Vasquez, D. W. (2003). Latinos in Rhode Island. *Gastón Institute Publications,* 97. https://scholarworks.umb.edu/gaston_pubs/97/

Walker, M. (2005). Amartya Sen's capability approach and education. *Educational Action Research, 13*(1), 103–110.

Werner, C. (2004). *Higher ground: Stevie Wonder, Aretha Franklin, Curtis Mayfield, and the rise and fall of American soul.* Crown Publishers.

Wright, B. L., & Ford, D. Y. (2019). Remixing and reimagining the early childhood school experiences of brilliant Black boys. *Boyhood Studies, 12*(1), 17–37.

Yosso, T. J. (2005). Whose culture has capital? A critical race theory discussion of community cultural wealth. *Race Ethnicity and Education, 8*(1), 69–91.

Zinn, D., Proteus, K., & Keet, A. (2009). Mutual vulnerability: A key principle in a humanising pedagogy in post-conflict societies. *Perspectives in Education, 27*(2), 109–119.

Index

The letter *f* following a page number denotes a figure.

About the Author

Carlos R. Moreno has been a teacher, a principal, and a director, and is now an executive director. A proud native New Yorker, Carlos is a passionate educational trailblazer committed to supporting school and district leaders to create high-quality, innovative schools designed to tackle systemic equity issues. He currently serves as co–executive director for Big Picture Learning, a nonprofit organization that has developed more than 200 such schools in the United States and around the world. He cofounded and leads the Deeper Learning Equity Fellowship, in partnership with the Internationals Network for Public Schools, and the newly created Ashé Leaders Fellowship. Carlos is also the founder and coproducer of the highly acclaimed Leadership Journeys storytelling initiative, which has featured inspirational figures such as Christopher Emdin, Dena Simmons, Kaya Henderson, Nancy Gutiérrez, Meisha Porter, Bettina Love, and Sharif El-Mekki. Carlos holds undergraduate degrees in marketing and business and a master's degree in educational leadership.

But those are merely Carlos's credentials. At heart, Carlos is an observer, a family man, a learner, a builder of community, a student, and a teacher—someone who has simultaneously found and continues to seek his own Leadership Soul.

Related ASCD Resources: Leadership and Equity

At the time of publication, the following resources were available (ASCD stock numbers in parentheses).

The Antiracist Roadmap to Educational Equity: A Systemwide Approach for All Stakeholders by Avis Williams and Brenda Elliott (#123023)

Becoming the Educator They Need: Strategies, Mindsets, and Beliefs for Supporting Male Black and Latino Students by Robert Jackson (#119010)

Cultural Competence Now: 56 Exercises to Help Educators Understand and Challenge Bias, Racism, and Privilege by Vernita Mayfield (#118043)

Culture, Class, and Race: Constructive Conversations That Unite and Energize Your School Community by Brenda CampbellJones, Shannon Keeny, and Franklin CampbellJones (#118010)

The Equity & Social Justice Education 50: Critical Questions for Improving Opportunities and Outcomes for Black Students by Baruti K. Kafele (#121060)

Five Practices for Equity-Focused School Leadership by Sharon I. Radd, Gretchen Givens Generett, Mark Anthony Gooden, and George Theoharis (#120008)

Fix Injustice, Not Kids and Other Principles for Transformative Equity Leadership by Paul Gorski and Katy Swalwell (#120012)

The Innocent Classroom: Dismantling Racial Bias to Support Students of Color by Alexs Pate (#120025)

Leading Within Systems of Inequity in Education: A Liberation Guide for Leaders of Color by Mary Rice-Boothe (#123014)

Leading Your School Toward Equity: A Practical Framework for Walking the Talk by Dwayne Chism (#123003)

Stay and Prevail: Students of Color Don't Need to Leave Their Communities to Succeed by Nancy Gutiérrez and Roberto Padilla (#123006)

For up-to-date information about ASCD resources, go to www.ascd.org. You can search the complete archives of *Educational Leadership* at www.ascd.org/el. To contact us, send an email to member@ascd.org or call 1-800-933-2723 or 703-578-9600.

The ASCD Whole Child approach is an effort to transition from a focus on narrowly defined academic achievement to one that promotes the long-term development and success of all children. Through this approach, ASCD supports educators, families, community members, and policymakers as they move from a vision about educating the whole child to sustainable, collaborative actions.

Finding Your Leadership Soul relates to the **safe**, **engaged**, and **supported** tenets. *For more about the ASCD Whole Child approach, visit* **www.ascd.org/wholechild.**

WHOLE CHILD
TENETS

1 HEALTHY
Each student enters school healthy and learns about and practices a healthy lifestyle.

2 SAFE
Each student learns in an environment that is physically and emotionally safe for students and adults.

3 ENGAGED
Each student is actively engaged in learning and is connected to the school and broader community.

4 SUPPORTED
Each student has access to personalized learning and is supported by qualified, caring adults.

5 CHALLENGED
Each student is challenged academically and prepared for success in college or further study and for employment and participation in a global environment.